·DANA CRAWFORD·

Published by the Upper Gulch Publishing Co.
P.O. Box 604
Denver, Colorado 80201

www.Uppergulchpublishing.com

ISBN 978-0-9963285-0-0 (hardback)

ISBN 978-0-9963285-1-7 (paperback)

Front and back cover photographs: © James O. Milmoe
Covers designed by Judy Anderson

Preceeding page:
The original 65-foot-tall "Welcome" Arch in front of Union Station facing up 17th Street. The other side of the arch also had the word "Welcome", which confused departing passengers as they arrived at the station. Mayor Robert Speer changed it to "Mizpah", a Jewish biblical term asking the Lord to watch over travelers. The 70-ton iron arch, erected in 1906, became a traffic hazard as automobiles became more popular, and was removed in 1931.

Photo by LC McClure, Otto Roach Collection

·DANA CRAWFORD·

50 YEARS

SAVING THE SOUL

OF A CITY

BY MIKE MCPHEE

Mike McPhee
10/1/15

————

To Barbara, with love

To my sister Melanie, for her courage and strength

And for my mother, Ursula, whom I never got to know.

————

*"We may appreciate the new,
but we value the old,"*

~ Shelley Don, entrepreneur, lawyer, thinker

"Who is that woman?" asked a friend of mine, staring at the figure leaning on the Union Station balcony rail. The elegant woman wore a multi-colored top and white pants, and as she laughed and gestured, her short-cropped silver hair gleamed and bounced in the late afternoon sun.

"That's Dana Crawford," I replied, realizing again how this 80-something-year-old woman can dominate a space.

She always has. In the early 1980s, when she would address the State Historical Society Board, which I served on as first lady of Colorado, the room would grow silent, hearing aids would be cranked up and pencils poised in mid air. No one wanted to miss a word of hers. She commanded absolute respect.

Dana never claimed her gender as an asset or a barrier on her journey to become the premier Denver visionary and historic preservationist.

Instead, she claimed her passion. "As a newcomer to Denver in 1954, I could see that its architectural history was about to be erased," Dana told me in 2012. "And I felt very motivated, almost obsessed, with a need to figure out a way to save at least one block of the 26 blocks in downtown Denver that were slated for demolition."

That passion led to the restoration and redevelopment of the 1400 block of Larimer Street, historically Denver's most important block which had become the heart of Denver's "skid row."

Dana's vision created Larimer Square, a gathering place unlike any other in the country, and turned a historical setting into a modern success story, one that still attracts locals, as well as visitors from all over the world, to enjoy themselves 50 years later.

Dana continued her vision by going where no one else dared, revitalizing old warehouses and remodeling them into elegant lofts and condos that drew people back to the city to live. Call her the midwife of Denver's LoDo.

These kinds of projects require team building, and team building requires a person who everyone trusts. The last four mayors of Denver all agree that no one did that better than Dana Crawford.

She was fearless, and found a way to solve problems. When the Larimer Square development was hindered by a bureaucratic law that said her four restaurants all had to be under "one roof" to obtain a liquor license, she wasn't fazed. She simply built a roof between the two buildings that housed the restaurants.

"I remember Dana Crawford when I arrived in Denver, in 1958," says philanthropist Lee Palmer Everding. "I think if she was born earlier she could have led the suffragettes or led the wagon train out west. She saw possibilities that others did not think about... She was active at a time when women had to use a side door to get into the University Club.

"Denver is the great city it is today partly because Dana Crawford had big dreams and acted on them."

Denver's expansive and colorfully renovated Union Station, the culmination of her career, contains The Crawford Hotel, named after Dana. Even though she first resisted her partners' suggestion to name it for her, at the groundbreaking of the hotel on Nov. 11, 2013, Dana showed that she was fully on board and in charge:

"A tremendous amount of thought has gone into every square inch," Dana said of the hotel. And, "I will be making sure the water is hot," she joked to Denver Post reporter Aldo Svaldi.

At a recent benefit for Planned Parenthood, held in the downstairs "catacomb" of The Crawford Hotel, Dana told of constantly being asked what else she and her late husband, geologist John Crawford, were doing in those early days of her preservation work.

"I just tell them, 'Well, we had four boys in a row, and then we joined Planned Parenthood!'"

Dana is constantly looking for ways to have fun, and some of her stories are legendary. To celebrate her 80th birthday, her youngest son, Duke, drove her through Italy for two weeks, visiting friends, dining and discovering.

Driving into Rome on their final night, they arrived too late to rent a hotel room. Dana insisted on Duke driving her around the rest of the night, without traffic, crowds or noise. Back at the airport, still with an hour to kill, she lay down in the back seat with her bare feet out the window and slept.

As author Mike McPhee said, "I knew from the moment I started this book that capturing this remarkable woman's story would be difficult and unpredictable. What an understatement! Putting her story down on paper has been like stuffing 10 pounds of potatoes into a five-pound bag."

I have known Mike and admired his writing for over two decades. This four-year effort to bring this lovely story to readers like you is clearly his best work to date.

Dana has saved the soul of this marvelous city of Denver and brought it into the 21st Century. It took her 50 years, and she did it with grace and style and intelligence and courage. No other city in the country has a story as remarkable and as meaningful as Denver's and Dana's.

At the re-opening of the 100-year-old Union Station, now upgraded with the namesake Crawford Hotel, on July 26, 2014, Dana beamed her signature smile and laughed. "Back to the Future!" she told the large crowd. "For the next 99 years, it's all yours."

Thank you, Dana.

DOTTIE LAMM,
Former First Lady of Colorado

ACKNOWLEDGMENTS

I am indebted to my editor, Jeff Leib, whose thoroughness and attention to detail was superb, as was his willingness to go back over and over again to get it right. The text is infinitely better because of Jeff's contributions. I also am indebted to the book designer, Judy Anderson, who set the tone for the printed text with such a creative approach to a difficult job. She was ably assisted by Alexandria Jimenez. And a strong thank you to Kalyani Fernando, who researched countless photographs, drawings, maps and graphics for the book. Her contributions were significant and important.

Melanie Simonet jumped right in when asked for her opinions and help with layouts, design advice and suggestions. Without being asked, she was up at dawn shooting photographs which opened all of our eyes with possibilities. Thanks to her husband, John Simonet, for his encouragement and friendship.

Susan Spann and Tom Kelley handled my legal work with sophistication and professionalism. Agent Sandra Bond provided meaningful advice, references and introductions.

Thanks to everyone at the Denver Public Library's Western History Department, including director Jim Kroll, Coi Dummond-Gehrig and Brian Trembath; and History Colorado's Stephen H. Hart Library and Research Center, including Melissa VanOtterloo. Thanks to Monica Brewer at The Denver Post, Julie Dunn, Dick Kreck, Dennis Gallagher, Tom "Dr. Colorado" Noel, and Stephen and Joyce Singular.

Special thanks to Shelley Don, for his insight, wisdom and friendship; to Dick Kirk for his friendship and support, and to his lovely wife, Susan, who died shortly before publication. Thanks also to the late Sen. Ken Gordon, with whom the early morning walks we took I will never forget.

To U.S. District Court Senior Judge John L. Kane Jr. for his sage wisdom and quick laughter, along with his wife, Stephanie; Joe St. Veltri, Harley Shaver and David Miller; to Gary Lozow, Hal Logan, Tom Overton and Mike Feeley; Tom Bidell and his wife, Jill Nelson, who listened attentively through many dinners to ideas and dead ends; same for David Milofsky's literary navigational warnings, and his elegant wife, Jean. To Clifford Beem, Danielle Beem, Christie Beem and Chris Ramos; the Hon. Richard Lamm, the Hon. John Hickenlooper, Helen Thorpe, Craig Truman and Bill Saslow. Many thanks to Arnold Grossman and Christie Murata for their keen insights, to Tom and Michelle Botelho and to Andrew Casalini and his refuge Satchel's on 6th Ave.

And finally to John Guare, who has mentored me through my entire writing life, giving me strength and courage I could never imagine; along with Will Adair, the third leg in our 40-year friendship.

TABLE OF CONTENTS

·MAP OF DANA'S LANDMARKS·

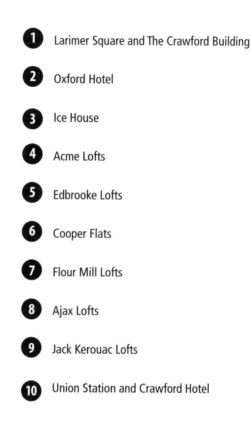

1 Larimer Square and The Crawford Building

2 Oxford Hotel

3 Ice House

4 Acme Lofts

5 Edbrooke Lofts

6 Cooper Flats

7 Flour Mill Lofts

8 Ajax Lofts

9 Jack Kerouac Lofts

10 Union Station and Crawford Hotel

· DANA'S WORLD ·

"I have become convinced that for a long,

long time this has been a series of struggles

supported occasionally by a few good laughs."

~ Dana Crawford / January 5, 2013

On a hot summer day in 1963, Dana Crawford walked out of her stylish brick home on Humboldt Street near the Denver Country Club, leaving her four young boys with their nanny.

She had started exploring various parts of Denver, looking for a space or a square or a cluster of buildings that she could turn into a gathering place—for socializing, for dining or shopping or for just getting out on the town.

"I had an idea about that from the day I arrived in Denver," she said. "It was so badly needed—a place where people with all kinds of backgrounds could get together and celebrate the city. There was nothing going on with preservation."

It was a vague idea that had been on her mind for years, inspired by farming towns of her childhood, by the college campuses she had lived on and the quaint New England villages she loved to visit.

"New England was filled with places for people to get out onto the streets," she said. "A big part of my interests developed there."

She had looked at a number of places in downtown Denver, like the old Metropole and Crest hotels on Broadway, and the area around the Exodus nightclub, where the Kingston Trio used to sing, near 20th Avenue and Lincoln Street.

On this day, she drove down Larimer Street, into the heart of the city's Skid Row. Jack Kerouac, in his epic 1957 novel, *On the Road*, depicted one of the book's pivotal characters, Dean Moriarty, as "the son of a wino, one of the most tottering bums of Larimer Street." Dean "used to beg in front of Larimer alleys and sneak the money back to his father, who waited among the broken bottles with an old buddy."

One of three paintings on the ceiling in an interior archway in Larimer Square by Evan & Brown, San Franscisco.

They lived in the old hotels near 17th and Larimer, like the Barclay and the Windsor, which had deteriorated over the years from chic elegance to "flophouses with a marble fireplace in every room."

Larimer Street was lined with cheap liquor stores, seedy pawn shops, dilapidated hotels and abandoned buildings, many of which had been reputable years ago but now were waiting for the bulldozers. Some of the recessed doorways held urine-soaked bums sleeping in contorted shapes, holding onto vodka bottles, most of them empty.

The area was so bad that the legendary beat cop, Harold "Swede" Schalbrack, a large man quick with his nightstick, would grab the drunks being tossed out of bars and throw them back into the same establishments that had created the problem by over-serving them. Swede's methods were controversial but effective because the streets undeniably were calmer and cleaner during his shifts.

Into this squalor drove a 32-year-old woman, a great beauty, an Ivy Leaguer and a Junior Leaguer, who joked that she had grown up with a silver spoon in her mouth, although her spoon had been empty. *The Denver Post* wrote that she resembled Jacqueline Kennedy. She was on a mission, a highly improbable dream that soon would teach her more about life than she ever imagined.

That mission started with car trouble.

The intense Colorado sun was baking the Ford's seats and steering wheel, and reddening Dana's lily-white arms and hands as she cruised Larimer. Waves of heat rose from the asphalt, which was beginning to soften.

Suddenly her Ford convertible coughed and sputtered. Dana pumped the gas pedal, which caused the engine to rev ever so briefly before it died. Flustered, she got out of the car and glanced around, hopelessly overdressed for the location and the situation.

"It's vapor locked," came a raspy voice from a doorway. "The engine's too hot."

Dana looked at the source, a group of winos in a doorway sharing the remains of a bottle and a cigarette. Hesitatingly, she asked them in her most helpless of voices what she should do.

Soon, a gaggle of men was under her hood, inspecting the engine. One of them found a rag, doused it in water and carefully wrapped the cool, wet cloth around the fuel line, which had become so hot that the gasoline inside had turned to vapor and choked the engine. A few more wraps of the cool rag, a twist of the key and the engine fired back to life.

From the driver's seat, Dana gave this ragtag group of men one of her disarmingly beautiful smiles and a twinkle of her bright blue eyes, a powerful gesture her mother had practiced to perfection back in Salina, Kansas, Dana's home town. The men seemed to feel that smile clear into their lonely hearts, and now they were proud as hell that they had been able to rescue such a lovely lady. She had made their day. They remained speechless as she drove away, waving them a big thank you and goodbye.

The 1600 block of Larimer Street, or "Skid Row" with the original Ginn Mill bar, 1633 Larimer, named for owner Jack Ginn; the Manhattan Restaurant, 1627 Larimer, one of Denver's most popular restaurants in the early 1900s; and the original Gart Brothers Sporting Goods store, 1643 Larimer, selling wooden skis. Denver Urban Renewal Authority demolished the block in 1972.

Photo Denver Public Library, Western History Collection, X-29648

A Denver police officer walking his beat on Larimer Street in Denver's Skid Row pours a fifth of whiskey into the gutter, to the disbelief of the men he took it from. Larimer Square was the start of a remarkable change in lower downtown Denver.

Denver Public Library, Western History Collection, Rocky Mountain News, June 19, 1950

Squalor inside the Barclay Hotel, 1700 block of Larimer Street, circa 1950. Once Denver's most elegant hotel, it deteriorated into "a flophouse with a marble fireplace in every room." It was demolished in 1960.

Dana chose the 1400 block of Larimer Street to launch her dream, primarily because of its architecture. When she went to the Denver Public Library to research the block's history, she knew she had struck gold because of its historical importance. It had been the site of Denver's first City Hall, the first post office, the first barbershop, the first saloon and possibly even the first whorehouse.

Carefully and quietly, she either purchased or gained control of all but 2 of the 18 buildings on both sides of the street. The banks wouldn't touch her restoration project, particularly with an inexperienced woman at the helm, and required that all loans be personally secured by key investors she found for the project. Dana was forced to take out a second mortgage on her home to swing the deal.

Seven months after she got control of the block, Larimer Square's first tenant—a banjo beer hall named Your Father's Mustache—opened its doors on Dec. 28, 1965, with a line of customers stretching around the corner. That was soon followed by the Bratskellar, The Magic Pan, the 1421 Club, Poor Richard's leather shop, Gusterman's Silversmiths, which is still there, and the Café Promenade, which became a legendary gathering spot for much of Denver's social elite.

Strip of buildings: The east side of the 1400 block of Larimer Street in 1963, just as Dana found it.
The building to the far left is the Granite Building.
The empty lot next to it was named "Noel Park" for Noel Congdon, an original investor, and historian Tom Noel. It now is the site of Capital Grille.

Some shops didn't do well and were forced to close. Some had trouble paying the rent, forcing Dana to hound the deadbeats, a role she never anticipated playing. Male landlords were expected to be tough, and rarely were criticized for hardball tactics. A woman was treated very differently, and soon the newspapers had dubbed Dana "The Dragon Lady" for her efforts to collect rent.

Dana was determined to make her dream come true, and opened several businesses of her own, including Victoriana's Jewelry and The Market, which remains open today. In her typical fashion, Dana wanted a food store, bakery and coffee shop on the block, but didn't know the first thing about retail food operations. So she and two friends traveled to New York City, where she had arranged for the three of them to be tutored by the staff at Dean & DeLuca for three weeks. They rented an apartment on Prince Street in SoHo, which turned out to be so full of cockroaches that Dana slept in her raincoat the first night, before finding another apartment.

Dana persevered and continued to grow, improve and manage the square for 21 years. She sold it in 1986 to the Hahn Co., which had purchased the Tivoli Brewing complex across Speer Boulevard a few years earlier.

By then she was deeply involved in historic preservation, both locally and nationally. She was a co-founder in 1970 of Historic Denver Inc., which was formed to save the Molly Brown House from demolition. She was elected to the board of the National Trust for Historic Preservation, which honored her with its highest award in 1995.

In 1980, she purchased the run-down Oxford Hotel, and, once again, entered into a business—hotel operations—which she knew nothing about. The economy was bad at the time, the hotel was not being marketed correctly and the Oxford, along with Dana and her partners, were forced into Chapter 11 bankruptcy not once but twice, which she later referred to jokingly as "Chapter 22." But there was a silver lining in those struggles. Dana was able to partner with Walter Isenberg and his Sage Hospitality, a highly successful hotel operator, that successfully remarketed the Oxford and led to the creation of The Crawford Hotel in a renovated Union Station in 2014.

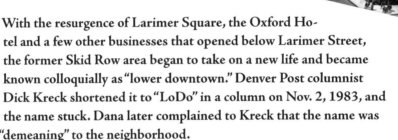

With the resurgence of Larimer Square, the Oxford Hotel and a few other businesses that opened below Larimer Street, the former Skid Row area began to take on a new life and became known colloquially as "lower downtown." Denver Post columnist Dick Kreck shortened it to "LoDo" in a column on Nov. 2, 1983, and the name stuck. Dana later complained to Kreck that the name was "demeaning" to the neighborhood.

Dana in a happy moment as Larimer Square begins to take shape in 1966.

Downtown Denver, including Union Station, in the early 1960s.

By the 1980s, Dana was developing a national reputation as a preservationist, eventually consulting for some 50 cities across the country. On these travels, she learned of other trends, some of which she brought back to Denver. In 1990, she pioneered the concept of renovating abandoned, brick warehouses into luxury lofts. Her first conversion was the Edbrooke Building at 15th and Wynkoop streets, followed by another conversion of the Acme Mattress Co. building at 14th and Wazee streets. Naysayers claimed no one would dare, or care, to live in abandoned warehouses down by the railroad tracks and Union Station. But Denverites loved the idea of living in wide-open "lofts" with few walls, ceilings 15' high braced with thick wooden posts and beams, and all within walking distance to most downtown offices. Other developers followed, and bidding wars broke out for windowless buildings filled with pigeons.

Once again, Dana's vision had been perfect. Some 30 years later, thousands of people are living between Larimer Street and the South Platte River.

Nothing was too insignificant for Dana to get involved in. When the Auraria higher education consortium failed to budget any money for landscaping its new campus, Dana found the money and had the grass, flowers, shrubbery and trees installed. She created the hugely popular Parade of Lights, held each year just before Christmas to raise money for the struggling performing arts community.

All the while, she was having fun. She imported two bright red, double-decker buses from London to carry tourists to Larimer Square. Her love affair with London led her to buy one of its ubiquitous black taxicabs, which she drove around Denver for years as her personal vehicle.

Over the past 50 years, no one has matched Dana Crawford's vision, drive and perseverance in shaping the future of downtown Denver. More than five decades after her "puke green" convertible quit on her in front of the winos, Dana and her partners have delivered to Denver a vibrant, activity-packed downtown that has won accolades from urbanists and preservationists throughout the nation and the world.

DANA'S WORLD | 9

DENVER'S MAYORS

Some of Denver's mayors made significant contributions, in part through their leadership and in part because of their authority and ability to fund large projects.

Mayor Robert Speer

Mayor Robert Speer joined the national "City Beautiful" movement in 1908 and contributed many of Denver's loveliest parks and forested parkways, starting with his eponymous Speer Boulevard.

Mayor Federico Peña

In 1983, Federico Peña was elected following his "Imagine a Great City" campaign, and his administration produced enormous results, including the cleaning up of the Central Platte Valley, removal of more than 30 sets of railroad tracks in the Valley, expansion of the convention center and work aimed at bringing Major League Baseball to Denver. Peña and the city had been hobbled by the 1974 Poundstone Amendment, which prevented Denver from annexing neighboring areas. Peña found a way around the constitutional amendment and grew Denver by more than 50 square miles, twice the size of Manhattan, on which Denver International Airport would be built. President Bill Clinton recognized his talents and tapped him after two terms as mayor to become his Secretary of Transportation, then Secretary of Energy.

Mayor Wellington Webb

Wellington Webb was elected mayor for three consecutive terms beginning in 1991, during which his administration accomplished a mind-boggling number of projects. Webb oversaw roughly 85 percent of the construction of DIA and he made the difficult decision to jettison the airport's expensive and fatally flawed automated baggage system. His administration championed construction of three sports venues for Denver's professional sports teams, all located in the Central Platte Valley, with easy access to public transportation. Webb helped spawn new communities on the sites of the former Stapleton Airport and Lowry Air Force Base. He tripled the size of the convention center.

Webb was a pragmatist and a doer, and let the lawyers and bureaucrats figure out the details.

On a handshake with developers in Seattle, Webb ensured the creation of Confluence Park, Commons Park and Cuernavaca Park, giving the first spark to what later would bring $500 million in transit improvements to the area around Union Station. The mayor also threw his support behind the Regional Transportation District's multibillion-dollar FasTracks plan to create a network of rail lines using Union Station as its hub.

IN THE END, THE MAYORS TIP THEIR HATS TO DANA.

"Dana truly was a visionary. She set up historic preservation in Denver.
There's no one else like her. She could be encouraging and extraordinarily
supportive one day and challenge you the very next. She's one of the few
who held on through the difficult times and she deserves credit for showing
us the importance of historic preservation."
~ Federico Peña

"Dana's hands are on everything in this city. She's been involved in every activity
related to downtown since I can remember, through her vision and her agitation.
So many of her projects were ones that everyone else gave up on and said they
couldn't be done, like Larimer Square. Dana's a gem."
~Wellington Webb

Courtesy, © James O. Milmoe, 2014

·KANSAS·

*"I was going to be named Dana
whether I arrived as a boy or a girl."*

*Dana Hudkins, age 8,
Salina, Kansas, 1939*

Both sides of Dana's family had done quite well through the 1920s. Her mother and father each came from middle-class families, were quite comfortable financially, well-educated and raised with solid Midwestern values of work, love and caring for those around them. But all of this would change dramatically with the Great Depression looming. Their lives were about to become scattered and unpredictable.

Granville Lee Hudkins, the paternal grandfather, lived in "Indian Territory" in Oklahoma before moving his wife and four children to Kansas in 1909. First living in Cawker City, he developed the town's utility system and pioneered the Chautauqua cultural program. Moving his family to Salina, he set up the G.L. Hudkins Ford Agency, the first Ford automobile dealership in Kansas. He was an early believer that mass-produced automobiles would change America's economy in ways that couldn't even be imagined at the time.

Courtesy, Crawford Collection

*G.L. Hudkins, 1905,
Dana's paternal grandfather.*

G.L. took his first delivery of two railroad carloads of Model T Fords on Oct. 26, 1911. A newspaperman wrote: "Mr. Hudkins needed no salesmen. His biggest trouble was getting the cars here fast enough for the buyers to drive them home. They were Model Ts, which sold for $395 delivered."

For years, the Fords seemed to drive themselves out of the agency's doors, and G.L. invested his profits in Salina real estate, buying a substantial house for his family as well as numerous commercial buildings downtown.

G.L. and his wife had four children. Dale, who would become Dana's father, was the youngest, born in 1902 in Enid, Oklahoma. He was always considered "an afterthought" since he was 19 years younger than his oldest sibling. When G.L. Hudkins retired in 1920, he and his wife and their three oldest children moved to Long Beach, California. Dale was still in high school and stayed in Salina with family friends, in part because "he was so ornery." Two years later, G.L. died in California while Dale was in college.

Despite the distance and lack of support from his family, Dale became a likeable and popular guy. He was high energy and although he might have been a tad ornery, he wasn't a troublemaker. He loved to explore and test, and poke and prod, always wanting to know exactly how thick the ice really was. He'd try anything once, even surfing down a river.

He was a good student, finished high school and enrolled at the University of Kansas, without much direction from his parents. Dale liked using his hands and seemed to have an intuitive knowledge about mechanics. He could fix just about anything and would spend most of his life around engines of one sort or another, first in cars, then tanks, airplanes and later in boats. He boasted, at age 10, that he could take apart a Ford and put it back together.

Dale was a guy's guy, a competent golfer, a heavy smoker and very popular at the 19th hole.

The maternal side of Dana's family was quite different. Captain William Dana, who fought in the Battle of Lexington in the Revolutionary War, married Mary Bancroft in Massachusetts and moved to Ohio in 1789. The government at the time was giving land away to anyone who would clear it and farm it. William and Mary Dana homesteaded a large tract of farming land along the banks of the Ohio River in Belpre (French for beautiful prairie), 14 miles downstream from Marietta, in what is now southeastern Ohio and across the river from Parkersburg, West Virginia. Back then, it was part of the Northwest Territory of the newly formed United States.

"William Dana is said to have burned the first brick made in the Northwest Territory," according to an account in the Ohio History Journal.

The Dana family, which became prominent throughout the region, grew so large it eventually built three, two-story farm houses and filled them with grandparents, aunts and uncles and many cousins.

Laurence Nye Dana, Dana's maternal grandfather, left the farm and settled in Joplin, Missouri where he worked as a journalist. He and his wife, Mary Curtis Henry, had two children, the oldest of whom was a daughter, Josephine "Jo" Henry Dana, born on Sept. 30, 1907 in Joplin, where she was raised. She blossomed into a great beauty and became an accomplished dancer before leaving to study English literature at the University of Kansas.

Dana Farm, outside of Marietta, Ohio, on the banks of the Ohio River, circa 1850. The large farm was homesteaded in 1789 by Dana's New England ancestors, one of whom fought as a Minuteman in the Battles of Lexington and Concord in 1775.

It was at KU that Dale Hudkins caught Jo's eye, perhaps because he drove a racy and very fast Stutz Bearcat sports car. Soon after graduating, the couple married in 1928 and moved to California, to be near his family in Long Beach. In California, Dale learned to surf and the young couple teamed with Dale's fraternity brother, actor and musician Buddy Rogers, who later married film star Mary Pickford, for many glamorous Hollywood outings.

But jobs were hard to find and a short time later the couple moved back to Salina, where Dale joined the Ford agency, now under new ownership. The couple built a large, new house in an exclusive area known as "The Hill". Life was good. But with the coming Depression, the neighborhood soon would be known as "Mortgage Hill."

Courtesy, Crawford Collection

The Hudkins family home at 620 Highland Ave., Salina, Kansas.

*Dana's parents'
wedding Sept. 28,
1928. Front row:
Josephine Bishop,
Dana's cousin;
Josephine Dana
Hudkins, Dana's
mother. Back
row: Best Man
Harold Garrett,
Dana's father Dale
Hudkins, Dana's
grandfather Lau-
rence Nye Dana,
and bridesmaid
Betsy Drake.*

Salina sits 100 miles southeast of the geographical center of the continental United States, in one of the largest wheat-farming regions in the world. The town's economy originally was based on farming, with its real financial strength coming later from flour milling. Agricultural transportation also played a significant role in the town's economy. In the early 1900s, four railroads laid tracks into Salina: The Missouri Pacific, The Rock Island Line, The Santa Fe and the Union Pacific. After numerous consolidations, only the Union Pacific serves Salina today, as well as several short-line railroads.

Interstate 70 clips the northern corner of Salina, extending 175 miles east to Kansas City and 450 miles west to Denver.

When long-range aircraft became important in World War II, the Army-Air Force built the large Smoky Hill Army Airfield outside Salina in 1943. The military based a number of B-29 strategic bombers there toward the end of the war. The field was re-organized into Schilling Air Force Base as part of the Strategic Air Command (SAC). Schilling was closed in the 1960s when missiles became the dominant weapon for national defense.

Boston Public Library, Print Department
(The Tichnor Brothers Collection)

Grain elevator along the Atchison, Topeka and Santa Fe Railway.

As the Great Depression squeezed the nation's economy, the Ford dealership was forced to close, leaving Dale without a job. He and Jo sold the house they had built on "Mortgage Hill" and moved back into the old family home downtown where Dale had grown up. He liked selling cars and soon found another job at the local Packard dealership, which survived the tough times.

Everyone was feeling the economic pressures. Jo tightened the family's purse strings and admitted later she had budgeted $1 a day for food for the three of them, boasting to Dana that "we always ate very well."

While food was always on the table, the luxury of acquiring booze had become nearly impossible because of the Depression and the waning years of Prohibition. So many families began making their own. Dale became quite adept at making bathtub gin, as well as beer, which frequently exploded while fermenting in bottles in the basement. Jo, the dancer, loved to party as did her gregarious husband, and their experiments with alcohol fueled the fun.

Photo: Denver Post, 1920

Prohibition stills, circa 1920.

Dale and Jo kept a positive attitude about life, despite the circumstances, and lived relatively comfortably thanks to Jo's frugality and Dale's ability to sell cars. Into this life of optimism, fun and bathtub gin arrived a much welcomed newcomer, Dana Hudkins, born on July 22, 1931.

Courtesy, Crawford Collection

Dana Hudkins, 1931
"I was going to be named
Dana whether I arrived as a
boy or a girl," she said with
a laugh. For reasons Dana
never understood, she wasn't
given a middle name.

At the time of her birth, it was a popular tradition to give the mother's maiden name as the child's first name.

"I was going to be named Dana whether I arrived as a boy or a girl," she said recently, with a laugh. For reasons Dana never understood, she wasn't given a middle name.

Perhaps because of her parents' gregariousness, or perhaps because the times were so perilous, Dana was given three godparents, each of whom grew to become an important part of Dana's life:

Dr. Brian Blades was a prominent local pulmonologist who stayed in close touch with Dana even after he was appointed head of surgery at the George Washington University School of Medicine, in Washington, D.C.

Margie Mize, a family friend and the great great granddaughter of Clement Moore, who wrote "A Visit From St. Nicholas," later popularized as the poem "'Twas the Night Before Christmas." Margie grew to prominence as a conservative and powerful legislator in Arizona. Her daughter became a close friend and sorority sister of Dana's at KU. (Another familial connection to the poem would be Dana's husband, whose great grandfather, Thomas Nast, was the cartoonist who illustrated the poem with today's popularly accepted image of Santa Claus.)

Margaret Sandzen, a close friend and sorority sister of Dana's mother. Her father, Swedish artist Sven Birger Sandzen, painted extensively in Colorado and became well known in the arts community of Colorado Springs.

Dana's parents weathered the Depression as well as most families, with Dale selling Packards first as an employee and later as the owner of a new Packard dealership, the Dale C. Hudkins Co. A 1937 article in the Salina Journal stated that the Packard Six (cylinders) sold for $795 to $910, while the Advanced Packard 12 (cylinders) could be purchased for $3,420.

Dana's childhood memories aren't of the hard times and difficulties everyone faced in the 1930s. Hers are of happy times, of drives with the family or shopping trips with her mother when they would have lunch in downtown Salina at the "Cozy Inn Hamburger" joint. They sat on two of the four stools at the counter, ordered tiny steer burgers which were sold "5 for 25 cents," and finished off with fabulous apple pie.

Dana says she can still smell the chicken pot pie at Peoples Cafeteria and the "best grilled-cheese sandwiches in the state" at Kresge's 5 & 10. These memories 75 years later still bring tears to her eyes.

She grew up an only child, a happy child with many friends. As she grew older, they became more and more important to her. "I never wanted to come home" from playing with them, she said.

Two of her most important friends were the Anderson sisters: Nancy (now Matthews) who would become publisher of the Tracy Press newspaper in Tracy, California; and Jody, who became a physician in Salina. Both their parents and Dana's parents had been close friends at KU. The Andersons later owned a wholesale fruit and vegetable business in Salina, which helped both families through the Depression. The families got together almost every weekend, always with much laughter, the kids recalled.

Nancy loved Dana's parents. Dale was "one of the funniest, craziest most wonderful people in the world." And Jo "was a beauty—elegant and shapely with the ultimate feminine look. She had big eyes that she would bat at you, not as a flirt but as a communicator. She never swore, she would just draw you into her circle. Dana learned that very well."

The Anderson girls were tomboys, who were taught to be independent and self-sufficient. Nancy said her parents put her on a train, alone, when she was 5 years old, to ride 110 miles out to her grandparents' home in Topeka.

Dana, on the other hand, modeled herself after her elegant mother, always wanting to please her and dress properly. So the stage was set one Christmas, when the Hudkins drove to the Andersons for a visit after church services. Dana was dressed appropriately in a blue suit, with black patent-leather shoes and a little navy blue coat, Shirley Temple-style, with white gloves.

Dana age 7, In her front yard.

"Jody and I were dressed in cowboy suits with guns and ropes. Dana came outside with us and my sister and I tied her to a tree and left her there," Nancy recalled. Despite their differences, the three girls remained lifetime friends until Jody died in 2014. A few months after Jody's death, Nancy flew to Denver to be with Dana at the grand opening of The Crawford Hotel in Union Station.

"Jody and I were dressed in cowboy suits with guns and ropes. Dana came outside with us and my sister and I tied her to a tree and left her there," *Nancy Anderson Matthews, Dana's childhood friend*

Courtesy, Crawford Collection

Dana's maternal grandparents struggled with the ravages of the Depression and in 1936 finally gave up their home in Joplin to move back to the security and comfort of the family compound on the Dana Farm. That prompted Jo to take her five-year-old daughter for her first visit to the pastoral enclave in Ohio. It opened up a new world for Dana.

"Dana Farm (became) a big part of my growing up. We went back there every year. I remember one summer, when I was about six, I got the chicken pox. Grandmother covered me with Vaseline, then wrapped me in a big heavy sweater so I wouldn't scratch. I think I still have some marks."

They owned, or at least had the use of, two Packards through the Depression and loved riding in them. Each summer, the three of them would drive to Colorado for a vacation, usually near Gunnison, to camp and fish. Dale, nicknamed "Catfish" back home because of his prowess with a fishing rod, would hook plenty of trout, which Dana loved to eat.

Dale Hudkins, age 22, 1924

Josephine Dana Hudkins, age 21, 1928

In America, despite the Depression, there were still reservoirs of hope and optimism. But much of the world was becoming unsettled and soon it would be engulfed in war.

In 1941, Dana was 10 years old and entering the fifth grade. She vividly remembers coming home from school one day to discover her parents packing up the house. Her father, anticipating the approaching war, had accepted a new, more secure job with Guiberson Motors in Dallas. The family's plan was for Dale to move alone to Texas while Dana and Jo would travel by train to Ohio to live at the Dana Farm with Jo's parents, known to Dana as Gran and Toddy.

Life in Ohio was a difficult transition for Dana, who understandably became lonely and insecure while wanting to be accepted in her new surroundings. She entered fifth grade at the elementary school in Belpre, where she was placed in the lower-achieving of two fifth-grade classes. This upset Dana tremendously because she had always worked hard in school trying to please everyone.

She also had a difficult time adjusting to the rule that boys and girls were separated during recess, unlike in Kansas. So Dana, used to having so many tomboy friends, decided to play with the boys during recess, which caused some commotion.

Another adjustment for Dana was being assigned homework, which never occurred in Kansas. But that imposition had a positive twist for Dana because it gave her mother the opportunity to help her with her school work, which drew them even closer together. "Mother also taught me how to type," she said.

Courtesy, Crawford Collection

*Dana Farm
in the spring*

Most of all, she remembers the loneliness of living on a farm. So, with her mother's guidance, she started exploring the family's large collection of books, which took her on new adventures with fictional characters as her friends. "That's where I got my love of books and antiques," she said while seated in her loft in Denver in front of a floor-to-ceiling wall of bookcases holding more than 1,000 books. "No one in Ohio ever threw away anything. I still have tons of stuff, like dishes, everything."

Another indelible memory of Dana's stay at the farm was watching her grandfather one Sunday morning lean in to the large, oval-shaped radio so as not to miss a single word. It was Dec. 7, 1941, and Japanese planes had just bombed U.S. warships docked in Pearl Harbor, Hawaii.

The nation was in shock. On the farm, three generations of Dana women began knitting warm stocking caps for the servicemen overseas. Dana's uncle Bill soon left the farm to join the Army and defend the country.

Amid the turmoil and fear of America going to war, Dana continued to study hard and do what she could on the home front to help her mother and her grandparents. At the end of the school year, the principal told her she had done so well that she would be moved into the "smart" class for sixth grade.

But to her surprise, her father suddenly showed up at the farm one day and told the family he had been transferred to Baltimore. There wasn't a lot of time to move and he wanted them to drive out there with him to find a house for all of them.

"We went out to Baltimore to find a place to live and stayed in an adorable house (bed-and-breakfast) in Havre de Grace," she said. "But we couldn't find a place to live. This was 1942 and there had been no building during the Depression. Now it was wartime and there was a heavy naval presence—Annapolis, submarine school, navy shipyards. Everything was crowded, the trains, everything. We couldn't find anything and I was nagging them to go back to Kansas."

Dale, who by then was 39 and too old to enlist, got frustrated with the gypsy life and the discomfort it was causing his wife and 11-year-old daughter. So he called his boss, quit his job and announced to Jo and Dana, to their great happiness, that they were moving back to Salina, where he was confident he could find work of some kind.

On the drive back to Belpre, Dana remembers only one thing—stopping somewhere and seeing a television set for the first time. At the farm, they gathered everything that would fit in the car and continued on to Kansas.

"In the fall of 1942, we returned to Salina for the 6th grade. I remember that drive, the car was packed to the gills with stuff. About 20 miles from Salina, I began to recognize things and remembered the smells. I started jumping around with joy. I was so happy we were going back to Salina."

While they had been gone, they had rented out their large family house in Salina. Upon return, they decided the rental income was so good that they left the tenants in the house. They built a one-bedroom apartment in the empty attic over the large, four-car carriage house in back. Once it was finished, Dana was relegated to sleeping on the sofa in the living room. "I stayed a lot with friends," she recalls rather dryly.

Dale quickly found work inspecting airplanes at the new Smoky Hill Army Airfield. He was happy, because of his love of machines and engines. But he learned that aircraft design and construction during the war was almost primitive and rudimentary. He never trusted their reliability. More than a decade later, when Dana was ready to go to college, he refused to let her fly and ordered her to take trains, even to Boston.

———

"We lived a meager life," Dana recalled. "A hunting friend of father's, Hugh Carlin, always brought us churns of cream. We all sat around churning butter, so we always had plenty of butter. The same man always brought us pheasants they hunted. So we always had plenty of food."

"Both my mother and father were fabulous cooks. It was from them that I picked up a love of food."

However, her mother had no patience teaching her to cook. "She tried once to teach me how to cook an egg but I dropped the first one on the floor. That was the end of that. She was very impatient but a total dreamboat," said Dana.

Courtesy, Crawford Collection

Dana, age 12, with Gay-Gay, the family's first dog, to the left and "Mike" to the right.

Dale began hunting and fishing with his friends, partly for the enjoyment and partly to add to the food on the table. Soon, he reasoned, he needed some hunting dogs, which they could hardly afford. So Dana and her mother convinced him that he could buy dogs if he gave up smoking and the cost of the tobacco. He agreed.

Their first dog was a Brittany Spaniel, named Gay-Gay, who was more of a retriever, soon to be followed by a Llewellin Setter, Mike, who ran forever, covering wide swaths of the hunting fields flushing out the birds. With two excellent bird-hunting dogs, Dale was popular as a hunting companion and Dana quickly developed her life-long love for dogs.

Gay-Gay soon was bred for pups. One day, with Dana home alone, Gay-Gay began to deliver the first of eight pups. Dana, who was barely a teenager, went into a near panic trying to find her parents. So she did her best and helped Gay-Gay deliver seven more pups. "I learned a lot about the birthing process that day," she said.

"Most of the adorable puppies were either sold or given away. But we kept two and unfortunately, tragedy struck. Mike and Gay-Gay came down with a distemper-like disease and died. The two puppies had been inoculated but they contracted the disease as well. One died and the female puppy struggled to survive. My mother held her close to her breast night and day, feeding her with an eye dropper until it was clear that the pup was going to make it," Dana said while tearing up. "We named her 'Baby Daughter'. Baby lived a long time and was a fabulously smart dog who became a great hunter."

The ruse of getting Dale to quit smoking to pay for the dogs didn't last long. "Soon, dad started smoking again," said Dana. "He chain-smoked heavily, 4-5 packs a day, for another 20 years, until he was 60. Then, one day he quit cold turkey. He lived until he was 83. Mother was also a life-long, heavy smoker. She died unexpectedly from a heart attack when she was only 55."

"I hated the smell of sulfur from the matches and the smell of smoke," Dana said.

"I didn't smoke at all in high school and constantly nagged at my parents to stop. But I started smoking almost the minute I left for college. There were several girls from Denver on the train to St. Louis; they taught me how to smoke."

The Junior Class of Salina High School
Presents

"Sixteen in August"

By
Dorothy Bennett and Link Hannah

Directed by Jack Kelly

★

Washington High Auditorium
December 12-14, 1946
8:00 p.m.

THE
1946 TRAIL
SALINA HIGH SCHOOL

PUBLISHED BY THE SENIOR CLASS

Football
Program

·COMING OF AGE·

On learning to drive at age 14,

"At that age, we were allowed only to run
errands for our parents. But...."

~ Dana Crawford / September, 2013

*Dana, age 14, enters
high school.*

*Dana with high school beau
John Eaton.*

Dana started high school in 1945, just as World War II was coming to an end. She was a happy, hard-working student who suffered a few setbacks but achieved a large number of successes. Overall, she was an "A" student and twice was named to the National Honor Society. Although she claims she actually loved algebra and trigonometry, her real passions would develop for writing and the theater.

She had two powerful role models in school, one an American History teacher, Edna Maude Smith, who also had taught her father the same courses in the same high school. The other was Jack Kelly, her drama and theater coach, who would carry her forward to winning "Best Thespian" in her senior year.

She was very popular, dated a lot for her age and enjoyed herself. "We had such a fabulous time in high school, so much fun," she said. Proof of that could be seen in her senior yearbook, in which the blank spaces were crowded with delightful, hand-written salutations from her classmates. Typically, most of them were syrupy and sweet, such as Sue Sykes addressing her as "Fizz," for her bubbly personality. Even her homeroom teacher, Mary Nielsen, wrote adoringly, although a bit more direct: "You are too lively at times but you suit me fine. You are a very dependable student and I wish you the very best that life can offer."

Dana partied a lot with her girlfriends and began to date a number of young men, of which there were plenty trying to catch her eye. By senior year, she had settled on one of the Big Men On Campus, John Eaton, a terrifically handsome guy who was the senior class treasurer and quite a jock. Their mutual admiration carried through graduation, with many yearbook salutations warning her "Hope you and John don't get into trouble at the commencement dance."

(Ironically, Eaton also would move to Denver after college, where he made a career with The Denver Post, first as assistant city editor and finally automotive editor. Eaton never forgot Dana and began spending time with her, treating her to dinners and such, while well into their 80s.)

She was a voracious reader, which she learned from her mother and her family of book collectors on the Dana Farm. Her mother was a member of the Salina "Current Literature Club," similar to the Fortnightly Club in Colorado in which women meet every other week, pick a topic to research and return two weeks later with some sort of report or story.

"Every year, the literature club would pick a different country, then study its literature, history and current issues," Dana said. "Mother would take me with her to the Carnegie Library. All the adult stuff was to the right, where she went, and the kids' stuff was to the left, where I went. I eventually read my way through that library."

Her love of reading expanded into a love of writing, of all kinds. She joined the student newspaper in high school, *The Yeoman*, and became so immersed in the entire process of putting out a newspaper that she even learned how to set type. "I wrote and wrote and wrote, all kinds of stuff. We had our own printing press and I learned to set the type, which was upside down and backwards. I never knew why I was so proud of that but I figured it would help me somehow, later in life, like in PR?" Or that ever-so-unique and necessary skill for reading newspapers over the shoulders of fellow subway commuters in Boston and New York?

She also worked on the school yearbook, *The Trail*, which proved to be a catchy name, as nearly every classmate began their commentaries: "So I guess the Trail ends here…Best of luck…"

JOHN EATON: Camera Club 3, 4; Class Treas. 4; Dram. Club 3, 4; Dram. 3, 4; Hi-Y 3, 4; Jr. Play 3, Prod. Staff 4; Stu. Coun. 1; Thespian 3.

By senior year, she had settled on one of the BMOCs (big man on campus), John Eaton, a gifted athlete and senior class treasurer.

Dana was a whirlwind of activity in high school. She sang two years in the Chorus, served two years in the Drama Club including one year on its production staff, she starred in plays in both her junior and senior years as well as in a musical her sophomore year. She served on the student cabinet twice, the Scholarship Team, Thespian Club, Pep Club, newspaper staff and others. During her sophomore year she was selected into the National Junior Honor Society and into the National Honor Society during her senior year.

Dana Hudkins' senior-class listing in the *The Trail* yearbook '49 showed her with a big smile, coiffed hair, a pearl necklace draped down a cashmere sweater and a thick, fat paragraph of activities listed below her name.

Throughout high school, she maintained an "A" average, seemingly without much anxiety but with a lot of effort, which pleased her teachers, her parents and Dana herself. Pleasing people, particularly those above her or in some position of authority, would become a high priority for Dana as she climbed the ladders of school and work. Her strong work ethic emerged early in her life and would serve her well.

The Trail, Salina High School

Dana's senior class yearbook photo

DANA HUDKINS: Chorus 1, 2; Dram. Club 3, 4; Dram. Club Play Prod. Staff 3, Cast 4; GAA 1, 2; Jr. Girls' Club 3; Jr. Play 3; Musicals 2; Nat. Jr. Honor Soc. 2; News Staff 4; Sr. Girls Club 4; Scholarship Teams 3; Thespian 3; YTC 3, 4, Cabinet 1, 2; Pep Club 4; Nat. Honor Soc. 4.

Dana never enjoyed sports, other than swimming, claiming she was too uncoordinated to be good at them. She didn't work during the summers in high school and spent much of her time at the Salina Country Club. She said she tried lessons in tennis but didn't do well. "I had no eye-hand coordination, plus the wind blows there all the time," she said.

Dana strove for perfection in everything she attempted, in large part to please her elegant and demanding mother. But on several rare occasions, her father's mischievousness would emerge, surprising not only her mother but even Dana as well. The first real evidence of her father's influence came during her American history class, taught by Edna Maude Smith.

Time Magazine published weekly current-event quizzes, which the school administration thought would be good for the student body to take. The quizzes were given to various classes at staggered times throughout each week. After the quizzes were scored, the students would discuss the correct answers with their teachers.

Dana, ever the perfectionist, learned off-handedly that the juniors took the quizzes early in the week, several days before Dana's class took them. She and her friends saw an opportunity here and arranged to get the correct answers from the juniors in time for her class' quizzes.

Of course, the well intentioned plan backfired. "When everyone in our class got 100% of the answers right, Ms. Smith knew something was wrong and threatened to flunk everyone in the class for the semester," Dana recalled. "I was so upset. I knew where she lived, so six of us walked to her house one day and 'fessed up. We told her we had cheated and told her how. There were four grading periods, so she said she would flunk the six of us for one grading period."

Getting caught at cheating had a profound effect on Dana.

Getting disciplined for cheating taught her an important lesson. "I was very upset, but you faced the music for something you had done wrong. In Kansas back then, honesty was very big, a very important value. Personal integrity was very important; it made a big impression on the people around you."

Out of that incident, Dana developed bedrock values that would carry her through some of her most challenging times in the rough-and-tumble world of real estate development and preservation. Always, her word was her bond, and her reputation throughout life would be solid and honorable.

Always, her word was her bond, and her reputation throughout life would be solid and honorable.

Tom Congdon, who risked his own money as one of the original investors in Larimer Square, said 50 years later: "We invested because it was Dana." And Walter Isenberg, her partner for more than 20 years in the Oxford Hotel and later in the redevelopment of Union Station, tells the story of their very first business agreement being written down on a cocktail napkin in the Cruise Room bar inside the Oxford. With Dana's word, there was no need for lawyers and contracts, Isenberg recalled.

The Junior Class of Salina High School
Presents

"Sixteen in August"

By
Dorothy Bennett and Link Hannah

★

Directed by Jack Kelly

★

Washington High Auditorium
December 12-14, 1946
8:00 p. m.

Possibly Dana's most intense passion in high school was for theater and acting. She credits her childhood friends, Nancy and Jody Anderson, who loved plays and acting, for introducing her to the world of drama. Jack Kelly, the faculty sponsor and drama coach, would become Dana's most influential role-model in high school and his name still brings tears to her eyes when she reminisces about him.

"He was such a fabulous teacher," she said. "All I learned in theater applied to almost everything I did the rest of my life."

Her first acting experience was in a summer production of Hansel and Gretel. "I played a witch, so I grew my fingernails long and painted them green. I loved it."

The acting bug began to grow for her in high school. "I got really, really involved in theater; I read all the Greek plays. We had so much fun there. The theater department was on the top floor, the attic, of the high school, with all the props and sets up there. We spent a lot of time up there."

Dana's first theatrical performance, directed by drama coach Jack Kelly, who instilled a strong, life-long love of the theater in Dana.

Her junior year, the theater department produced *Death Takes a Holiday*, in which Dana not only acted in the play but helped direct it as well. It was a huge success.

Her senior year, the theater department put on the play *My Sister Eileen,* which really excited Dana. It was based on a series of stories in The New Yorker Magazine about two sisters from Ohio who move to New York. Eileen struggles to become an actress while the older sister, Ruth, wants to become a successful writer.

"My great friend Janie Floyd got the part as Eileen. I wanted the role of the older sister so badly that I went over to Jack Kelly's apartment one day and pleaded with him. 'Jack, I really want that role,' I said to him with my hands clenched together on my chest. He gave it to me."

DEATH TAKES A HOLIDAY: In her junior year, Dana not only starred in this romantic drama but also helped direct it.

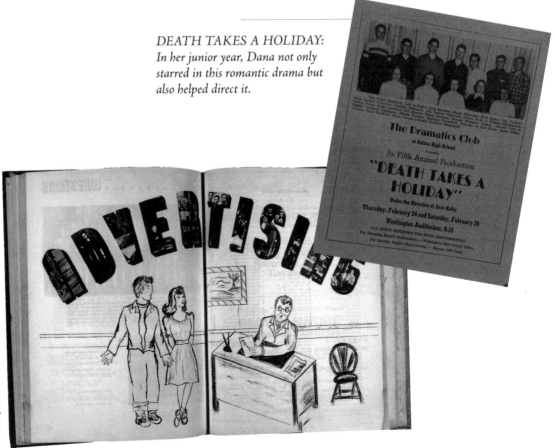

The production was a huge success and the local paper considered it one of the best productions ever in Salina. Her classmates voted her not only "actress of the year" but also "Best Thespian."

Drama coach Jack Kelly wrote two full pages in her yearbook, calling *Eileen* "the biggest success in the history of Salina High School." He said coming over to his apartment to lobby for the roll in *Eileen* was the right thing to do. "I'm glad you did."

"I was afraid the play would never shape up but it did…and I am afraid that without your experienced help as a steadying influence in the cast it wouldn't have…You were a marvelous 'Ruth'. Here's to my Best Thespian of 1949 and a person I am happy to call a personal friend. Love, Jack Kelly."

Reminiscing about Kelly and her successes in high school theater brought both smiles and teary eyes to Dana…the happiness and innocence of days gone by. She stared into the distance: "He used to run down the aisle and jump up onto the stage. I wonder if he still does?"

Dana and her theatrical "sister" Janie Floyd starred in the senior class rendition of the hugely popular comedy, which was based on a series of autobiographical stories in The New Yorker. Dana's classmates voted her "actress of the year" and "Best Thespian." Drama coach Jack Kelly called it "the biggest success in the history of Salina High School."

Surprisingly, Dana has mixed if not contradictory memories of high school.

> "I had to get out of Salina after high school. I wasn't very well liked," she said. Asked to explain, she said: "I was never voted in for anything, not a queen, even a princess. I was arrogant, which I learned from my mother."

Yet her melancholy is strongly contradicted by a pass through her yearbook, where she virtually carried the theater department, was voted "Best Thespian," worked on the yearbook, was elected to the student council and on and on. She even recalled one day in an interview for this book: "I had lots and lots of friends, lots of guys to go out with, lots of cars."

Some classmates believed Dana suffered because of jealousy from others. Ramon B. wrote in Dana's yearbook that she was one of the most wonderful persons she's ever known, but continued that a lot of classmates didn't like Dana, mostly because of jealousy.

Dana graduates from Salina High School, Spring 1949.

Her lifelong, childhood friend, Nancy Anderson Matthews, sympathized. "Dana told me she never felt popular. I think that would be true," said Nancy. "She told me she was never voted queen, that she resigned from student council because it wasn't important, and so on. It makes me think her expectations were too high."

Nancy continued: "Going through school, I could never stand the cliques that formed. I don't know if Dana wanted to be part of that. I wanted to be friends, but not part of the cliques. If you go into a group, they gather for protection. I grew up being challenged all the time so I never felt I needed protection. Dana was an only child and wasn't used to being challenged. Dana was so pretty, so nice, except for her acerbic tongue."

Dana shrugs it off. "Maybe I wasn't as nice as I should have been. I didn't really care about it."

Melancholy has a way of sneaking into our minds, caused by some unfulfilled expectation or disappointment. Memories on the surface, or from yearbooks and letters, seem to contradict the gloominess. But the memories for her remain very real.

·COLLEGE LIFE·

"Well, nobody wanted to marry me,

so I applied to Radcliffe,"

~ Dana upon graduating from KU with a BA but without an M-r-s.

"At Harvard, they taught us how to drink martinis.
When they asked me, 'Olive or onion?'
I had no idea what they were talking about."

Dana surprised many of her friends and classmates when she decided not to take the conventional path of enrolling as a freshman at the University of Kansas. Instead, she enrolled at Monticello College, a small, two-year private women's college in Godfrey, Illinois, about 20 miles east of St. Louis. The school had always been thought of as a "finishing school" for young women but Dana defended it as also being academically rigorous.

"Everyone was shocked when I chose to go to Monticello instead of following everyone to KU," she said. "Some of my mother's sorority (Pi Beta Phi) sisters were horrified that someone would send their daughter off to the East (St. Louis.) They assured her I would never get into a sorority. Mother said, 'we'll take the risk.'"

It was her mother's choice that she go to Monticello instead of KU, and Dana didn't object or rebel. "I think my mother was really good about not letting me get hung up with the teenage thing of everybody's doing it,' like riding in the back of an open truck," she said. "I was not to do that, that wasn't part of the Hudkins' and Danas' plan. We did things the way we thought was right."

So off she went, unaccompanied by any friends or classmates, to a junior college with a student body smaller than the high school she had just graduated from. She also had received a $400 scholarship for two years.

Monticello College

Benjamin Godfrey, a Mississippi River boat captain, founded Monticello in1838 as a female seminary for his 8 daughters. According to school lore, he believed that educating one woman would change the whole family. The seminary evolved into a junior college for women in the late 1800s. Lined with large, century-old deciduous trees, the grassy campus frames a collection of beautifully ornate Victorian buildings, mostly made of limestone, including the Benjamin Godfrey Memorial Chapel, an exceptional example of Greek Revival architecture, which was added to the National Register of Historic Places in 1979.

The school was sold in 1970 to the Illinois state educational system and renamed the Lewis and Clark Community College, a tax-supported junior college for men and women. The school sits about 20 miles from where the Missouri River flows into the Mississippi River, where Lewis and Clark began their epic exploration of the western U.S.

Dana had a difficult time adjusting to living away from home for the first time. "I hated Monticello when I came home for Thanksgiving the first year. That's common, I think. Nobody likes any school away from home at first. But by Christmas, I loved it," she said.

Life at the tiny, 350-girl school was quite different than in the large universities. The biggest difference was the absence of male classmates, which proved to be huge advantage for 19-year-old girls at their peak of self-consciousness, insecurity and distractibility. It relieved them of a lot of social pressures and anxieties. And when they wanted to be with the opposite sex, the girls had no trouble finding them.

"The two years I was at Monticello I had six dates, none of them repeats. We had parties and dances. There were other girls' schools, like Stephens (College in Columbia, Missouri) and Lindenwood (School for Girls in St. Charles, Missouri) and we all competed for the boys at the military academies and other schools. But it was very easy for me to forget about dating then."

Monticello emphasized academics by requiring the students to take difficult courses they might not have taken at a university until their third or fourth years. "I had to take chemistry (as a freshman), which was very hard for me. I wasn't good at science, but I finally managed to get an A," she said.

It also emphasized the finer points of a social education, requiring the women to take many "polite" classes unheard of at state universities. "We were taught manners, about everything," Dana said. "I learned about hosting parties, preparing hors d'oeuvres and putting on special events."

She also had to work on campus, first at the school's post office and later in the school's kitchen, where she learned how to prepare large quantities of food since everyone ate their meals together in a dining hall. The women were seated at round tables, 10 to a table, with student servers and clearers. Dana remembers the "fabulous" mashed potatoes and the huge machine in the kitchen that mashed them.

Dana grew very comfortable and secure within the school's structure and she began to excel. She was methodical about keeping a scrapbook, a thick, bound book in which she glued all sorts of momentos like invitations, announcements, report cards, dance cards and letters from home.

Not surprisingly, she was a straight "A" student, made the Dean's List and rose to the top of her class of 174 women. Toward the end of their first year, her classmates elected her class president for next year.

She still takes to heart some advice she got from the school's academic dean, Mary Laing Swift. "I never forgot a speech she gave at the start of the year," said Dana. "She said simply, 'Save your five minuteses.' There's so much you can get done if you focus for just five minutes.

I still do it.

"My second year, I had two roommates who were twins from East St. Louis—very thin, like fashion models. They were also class officers with me. We lived in a suite, which was really cool. We all went to St. Louis a lot for cultural stuff, the symphony, the art institute. I loved St. Louis because it was very historic. It became my second city."

Dana, right, elected senior class president. Behind Dana: Roberta Peoples, vice-president; Jean Stolle, Secretary; June Stolle, Treasurer.

That same year, she was chosen as one of seven women who "typified Monticello's ideals." A large, formal photograph in her senior yearbook showed Dana representing the ideal of wisdom—"the union of knowledge and understanding." She was selected as a charter member and vice-president of Monticello's first chapter in Phi Theta Kappa, the honor society for junior colleges. At commencement, she gave one of the summation speeches and was graduated with "highest honors" in the spring of 1951. "Monticello was a very formative experience for me," she said. "I had very good teachers."

Graduation Day, Monticello College, 1951. Dana, left, with Roberta Peoples.

Dana, center, in formal gown.

Dana began a metamorphosis in college, growing out of her high-school insecurities into a belief in herself and her abilities, her social skills and her desirability as a friend and confidant. The changes became quite noticeable the summer after she returned home from her first year at Monticello.

Dana's father had grown tired of selling cars and became fascinated with a new reservoir, Kanopolis Lake, formed after WWII when the Army Corps of Engineers dammed the Saline River about 35 miles southwest of Salina. Looking back on his father's accurate predictions about the developing market for Ford automobiles, Dale saw a similar market developing for boating on the 29-mile-long lake. He contacted the manufacturer of one of the most sought-after boats of the day and landed the first franchise in Kansas for Chris-Craft runabouts and small cabin cruisers. These sleek, varnished mahogany boats came with throaty inboard engines that made them thrilling and fast. They were perfect for the large reservoir and Dale was thrilled to get the exclusive distributorship.

Initially, he began running boating excursions and soon established the Kansas Boat and Motor Co. A friend who owned a beer distributorship nearby had space in his warehouse for Dale's new company, and the jokes soon came rolling in about a match made in heaven—one-stop shopping for a boat and some beer. Soon, he recognized the need for launching and docking these new boats so he built the first marina. Recreational boaters were flocking to the lake, particularly on weekends. The new reservoir proved to be a rich spawning ground for fish of all kinds. Soon the fishermen were arriving, needing all kinds of equipment and service, which Dale was only too happy to provide, beer included.

The marina grew so fast that Dale could barely keep track of it. It had started with boats and fuel. Now it was selling ice cream, hot dogs, souvenirs, boating equipment, books, charts and all kinds of fishing gear.

Courtesy, Crawford Collection

Dana, home for summer after her first year of college, wanted to work and asked her father if she could help. He was stretched so thin running the business, and Dana had become so dependable that he immediately put her in charge of keeping the books for the mushrooming business. He called a friend, Ralph Ritz, an accountant in a large firm in Salina, who readily agreed to teach Dana how to set up the books for the boat company. Dana caught on quickly, and worked hard at keeping track of the family's income—at the tender age of 19.

There's an old adage among boat owners that "any two boats traveling in the same direction automatically becomes a race." Soon there were boats going everywhere, so large races were organized for the summer holidays. They proved so popular that non-boaters started coming out to watch from the banks and beaches. The spectators got thirsty and hungry, so Dana and her father got a food trailer, which Dana ran on the beach. It made a lot of money for them, and Dana recorded it all in the books.

"Dad and I would take these big seines into the creeks and marshes where we caught all kinds of minnows. I ran the minnow tank, which was very educational," she joked sarcastically while rolling her eyes. Dana liked to fish, but wasn't a purist and found nothing wrong with baiting a hook with slices of hot dogs.

It didn't matter what was needed—Dale and Dana would find a way to provide it, even if it was live bait that the fishermen wanted.

Dale's marina on Kanopolis Lake couldn't keep up with the demand, and soon they built a concession stand which kept everyone busy.

The summer flew by for Dana, overloaded with work. In a letter to classmates at Monticello, Dana summed up her summer: "I've been working for my father at the marina on Lake Kanopolis. It doesn't give you much spare time for a love life or letter writing or even taking a bath."

Dana had learned to drive farm equipment when she was only 7. So learning to drive the runabouts was easy for her as a teenager, and soon she was taking guests out on excursions. But her father worried about the liability of taking paying passengers out on the water. So he told her she had to get a Coast Guard license. When she returned to the lake from Monticello, the season was already beginning to pick up. They would have to leave right away for St. Louis where she would take the test.

"I had no time to study at all for the test. We were in a panic. I remember we went downstairs in our hotel and hailed a cab to take us to the Custom House. He yelled at us.'Are you crazy? It's only one block away.' Oh well."

Dana's father had become very proficient with boats, and tried to give Dana a cram session on the drive to St. Louis. "I remembered that port was shorter than starboard, and left was shorter than right. So I put the two short words together.

"Inside the testing office, we sat at a table." If she was unsure of an answer, "Dad would tap his foot on mine twice if the answer was yes, and only once if it was no. I got my license!"

Courtesy, Crawford Collection

Dale Hudkins starts the first Chris-Craft dealership in Kansas, on Kanopolis Lake, a reservoir built after WWII. Dana gets her Coast Guard license, with her father's help, and pilots groups of cruisers. And she soon rivaled her father at catfishin'.

At the end of her second hectic summer working at the marina, Dana enrolled at the University of Kansas, in Lawrence.

It was quite a change for a small-town girl who had spent the past two years at a tiny, all-girls junior college. KU had a student body nearly as large as the population of Salina. And it had men, some 7,000 of them, with most looking for a mate. And it had dozens of fraternities and sororities, all of them in party mode.

In the early 1950s, marriage was a high priority for most students. Coeds joked that by the time you graduated, an "M-r-s." title before your name was just as important, if not more than a "BA" or "PhD" after your name.

"I seriously chased boys at KU. In those days, you had to get married," she said. "I also started to drink beer. I never liked it but it was so fashionable that I drank a lot of it."

She also pledged into the Pi Beta Phi, her mother's sorority and the one Dana considered to be the best on campus. With her stellar background from Monticello and with her mother's pedigree, she was quickly accepted.

Several of Dana's classmates from Monticello also came to KU and also pledged Pi Phi. "We were very close. We were at an advantage because we'd already been together for one or two years. (House mother) Aunt Elfie called us the "hood and Levi" crowd because we were always wearing Levi's and hoodies. It was very much against the rules for dinner."

In her sorority yearbook, Dana's profile read: "Sophisticated Dana is never without an idea and is often a great help to her pledge sisters. She holds the undisputed record of latest to bed and latest to rise."

Dana became quite popular among the fraternity men, and soon was "pinned" by Wally Beck of Phi Gamma Delta. Getting pinned was an important tradition in college at the time because it raised a woman's social status among her sorority sisters. John Eaton, her high school beau, was also at KU but Dana said that relationship had slowly faded away.

Despite her full social calendar, Dana remained dedicated to her studies, and some courses in the upper classes were quite a bit more difficult than she had imagined.

"I was required to take Principles of Physical Science, which I struggled with and got only a B, which was a huge disappointment. I never understood the principle of displacement of water."

Her natural tendencies toward leadership also began to grow. She thought the university should have better professors, and took it upon herself to tell the new chancellor, Franklin Murphy, a 35-year-old surgeon, how he might improve the university.

Understanding Dana's well intentioned though somewhat naïve remarks, Murphy told her it was more difficult than most people imagined to spend taxpayers' money on academics, especially during the Cold War. Kansans in the 1950s were fine with paying for more buildings but hiring better and more expensive academic professors was difficult. "The farmers thought they were all communists," Dana recalled the chancellor telling her.

Dana also got involved with theater and in January of her first year at KU was named director of the university's annual musical play *Strike a Match*, a musical spoof written, directed, performed and produced entirely by students. The show was a light-hearted poke at the difficulties and foibles of dating in college, of striking up a match. It had more than a dozen songs, all written and performed by students, including "A Coke Date":

"A Coke date, it's a great convention.

If you have the right intention.

It might lead to a long extension,

Of cuddling, snuggling, all types of struggling."

Dana and her crew put an enormous amount of time into preparing the show, including designing all the sets, the costumes, the publicity, ticket sales and rehearsals. She loved it, not just because it was theater but also because it was feeding her growing need to be in charge. All went well, so well that Dana felt confident enough to invite her theater mentor from high school, Jack Kelly, to Lawrence for the play and cast party that followed. Kelly quickly accepted such an important invitation and was in the audience on May 2, 1952.

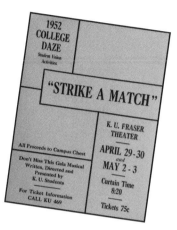

Dana, left, was picked to direct KU's annual musical, Strike a Match, about the foibles of dating in college.

Back home for the summer in Salina and working for her father at the marina, Dana's burgeoning love of writing gave her the confidence to approach the editor of the Salina Journal to let her write a column about life out at the lake, titled "Reservoir Ramblings." He agreed to give it a try. The columns had a folksy, newsy feel. Like any good columnist, she filled them with locals' names, to the point it became required reading among town folk and gave the marina a level of publicity that no amount of paid advertising could equal.

"I seemed to have a bent for public relations," she said. "But at the time, I didn't even know that field existed."

RESERVOIR RAMBLINGS

One particularly literary entry read: "This week's full moon and fallish (sic) breezes have invaded Kanopolis Lake to give it that resort atmosphere…. That old man in the moon has been strutting his stuff for the benefit of the lake's night fishermen…"

"He's Corporal Bob to the Marines but he is and always will be Captain Bob to us at Kanopolis Lake. It's mighty fine to have Bob Serrault home on leave from Korea."

"Mr. and Mrs. George Sauers and Mr. and Mrs. Robert Powers came home from a vacation in Colorado and discovered that the fishing was plenty good right in their own back yard. Mrs. Powers caught a five-pound flathead using a salmon egg on a spinner, left-overs from trout fishing in Colorado."

Summer fun on Kanopolis Lake.

Dana declared her major at KU to be educational studies, with the goal of becoming a teacher, exactly as her mother had "requested." But during her senior year, the Dean of Academics pulled her aside and explained that her exceptional academic record would qualify her for the honor society, Phi Beta Kappa, if only she were a liberal arts major.

So she made the switch to an English Literature major, with an emphasis on social studies and human relations. But a new major required her to take additional courses, more than she could handle.

"The last semester, I took 21 hours," she said. "They made me drop a three-hour class which I had to make up that summer."

She complained that summer school would prevent her from graduating with her classmates. So the school acquiesced if she promised to take a summer correspondence course. She agreed and was allowed to graduate on time, with her classmates, and as a member of the Phi Beta Kappa Honor Society. Coincidentally, she had done so well in her previous major in education that she also was elected into Pi Lambda Theta, the national honors society for education majors. Overall, Dana had been elected into national honor societies at every level: high school, Monticello and two at KU.

She returned home to Salina and her work at the marina and selected a correspondence course on the author Thomas Wolfe. "I just fell in love with Thomas Wolfe," she said. "It was magnificent to be immersed in his stories for an entire summer. I wrote these glowing reports about him and got a good grade. But the professor wrote in my final paper that as I got older, I probably wouldn't remain so enchanted with Wolfe."

———————————

Despite her academic successes, she was still single, with no real prospects of marriage and with no plans for the future.

But just before she graduated, opportunity knocked.

"I had been waiting for a professor one day when I saw a sign that Radcliffe College was looking for business administration graduate students," she said. "I mentioned it to him. He said he had gone to Harvard, that I should apply and he would write a letter for me."

"Well," she sighed, "nobody wanted to marry me after college, so I applied to Radcliffe. I needed a full scholarship, which I told them in the application. I was accepted, with a scholarship ($600), into a class of about 80 women for the fall of 1953."

We're not in Kansas anymore!

Dana had been in a whirlwind the past two years at KU, doing what she loved but without any grand plan. The Radcliffe graduate program came upon her as fast as the tornado in *The Wizard of Oz*, and swept Dana out of Kansas and into the exalted Ivy League charms of Cambridge, Mass., where she encountered infinitely more sophisticated classmates (just ask 'em), evermore challenging studies, two richly rewarding work internships, a charming social life and even a broken nose on Valentine's Night.

She found herself, once again, on an eastbound train, alone, without her classmates or friends, to another unknown, and very distant, college. She entered Radcliffe College, the female sister school to then all-male Harvard University, in the fall of 1953 for a one-year graduate program (no degree) in business administration and personnel.

The program wasn't just academics. In addition to six months of course work, it required completing two work internships. She chose one in retail sales at the B. Altman & Co. department store in New York City and another in public relations at the newly founded Museum of Science in Cambridge.

The official Radcliffe description stated: "The management training program is a one-year graduate course in personnel and business administration, designed to train young women for junior administration positions in business, industry, government, social service and educational institutions." It was to be taught, "for the most part," by members of the Harvard Business School faculty.

> "Harvard back then wouldn't admit women, even though we took the same classes from the same professors and studied the same cases as the Harvard Business School did across the (Charles) river," Dana said. "Harvard's excuse for not letting women into the business school was that they shouldn't have to listen to all the men's bad language."

"We argued that we were over there all the time. Every day after classes we'd go across the river and start drinking martinis with the men. I had a tough time learning the finer points. The first time they asked me if I wanted an olive or onion, I had no idea what they were talking about.

"When I got to Harvard, all the fancy, yacht-club men would ask me, 'Where did you prep?' I'd say, Salina High School. 'What business is your father in?' I'd say, we're in the boating business, in Kansas. There was always much laughter," said Dana.

"It was a fabulous educational experience. They used the case method. You learned to think, to make judgments and to take risks. For example, an insurance company wanted to increase production among its office workers. One of the workers is a troublemaker. We all divided into teams of 5 or 6 women, one would be the team leader, to solve the problems. After studying and talking, the teams would present their solutions. One might be to replace the troublemaker, one might bring in a consultant from outside. We'd have eight different solutions, which were boiled down to The Solution."

"I learned that it was OK to have different solutions," she said. "It was OK to collaborate instead of compete. And it was OK to be passionate about your solution. They encouraged the entrepreneurial spirit."

"And it created an attitude. They had told me not to let the 'Pinch Nose Yankees' get me down. But I became one!"

The one-year program earned Dana only a certificate of completion. A few years later, Harvard opened its business school to women and told former Radcliffe business students they could come back for another year of courses and receive an MBA from Harvard, which Dana chose not to do.

"I just fell in love with Boston; it's a strong influence with me to this day. I loved Newbury Street in the Back Bay. I loved shopping there. I loved downtown and Filene's Basement," she said.

In November 1953, Dana moved to New York for her six-week internship in retail sales with B. Altman. "I joined 'the flying squad' and was trained to be either a buyer or a department head," she said. "But I never knew which department I would be working in next. My first assignment was in housewares. The next day, I was assigned to the linens department, then handbags.

"An ad in the newspapers listed all sorts of stuff that we didn't have. I spent days making excuses, saying we would get it. I made a friend in the stock room, Louie, who I was constantly asking, 'Do we have this? Do we have that?' People kept coming in with the ads."

Dana's love of the theater flourished during her time in New York, where she managed to find tickets to Broadway classics like *Porgy and Bess*, *The King and I*, *Picnic* and *The Seven Year Itch*. And she found a sorority sister in New York, who took her to many parties, meeting "mostly men who were there without their wives."

She loved what she called the "quaintness" of Greenwich Village. "The creepy people who populate the village are fascinating to observe and overhear," she wrote in a letter to her mother. "The Young Intellectuals of America who never cut their hair! God only knows what horrible piece of modern art lies unborn beneath those uncombed heads."

In another letter to her mother, she wrote: "I learned you had to be rich to live in New York, and if you fell down on your face in the subway, Bostonians would step around you but New Yorkers would step on you."

For Christmas vacation, still not allowed by her father to fly, she rode the New York Central Railroad's Knickerbocker Express, pulled by steam locomotives, from New York to St. Louis. Another train ride brought her home to Salina.

Back in Cambridge in early 1954, Dana remembers clearly a blind date she accepted on Valentine's Day. He arrived drunk, continued drinking and soon crashed his car into an embankment on Massachusetts Avenue. Without seatbelts, Dana hit her face on the dashboard, breaking her nose and loosening some of her teeth. The dentist for Harvard's varsity hockey team fixed her teeth and a medical student stitched up the gash on her right cheek.

She didn't eat solid food for a week but the Harvard B-School men talked about what a good sport she had been through her trauma, which cheered her up. The worst part of the accident was that her injuries caused her to lose a six-week internship with NBC in New York. Instead, she found an internship with the Museum of Science, which had recently been established by explorer and mountaineer Bradford Washburn. (Washburn's family would make significant contributions to Colorado College and Colorado Springs, and helped establish the Bradford Washburn American Mountaineering Museum in Golden).

Dana was assigned to the museum's PR department, where her first assignment was to set up a reception for the famed mountaineer, Sir Edmund Hillary, who had become the first person to summit Mt. Everest just nine months earlier.

Heublein, the liquor company, had agreed to sponsor the reception, and provided the crowd with free martinis and Manhattans.

"My job was to put a cherry in the Manhattans and an olive in the martinis," Dana said. "Brad (Washburn) came up to me during the reception and asked me if I wanted to meet Hillary. I was enthralled that I would get to meet this tall, craggy man, which I did. Brad was so sweet the way he treated all of us."

Other duties at the museum included raising money for various museum activities, extensive writing assignments and other PR work.

Monday
March 28, 1955

Dearest Mamacita and Papacita –

The package is here with all its
happy surprises. The ...
but not all the fun t...
wonder ... 'ntil, di...
How ... ...
that ...
now ...
any...
mos...
is ...
beginning ...

little

sweet

Panorama from the Air
of the Civic Center and Business District,
Denver, Colorado

Skyline of Denver, Colorado

UNITED
STATES
POSTAGE

Dearest Mother and D...
calling me on Sun...
wonderful to hear y...
sounded much better!
previous conversati...
gone? The new car so...
and I know you'll...
in your many trips...
There really is...
on this end of the li...
week-end was restful...
off on Tuesday for ...
... I shall miss ...
... sence. They h...
... e to me.
... I reread the...
... doesn't make...
... lame it on to...
... lunch with ...
... Annabelle to...
... time for a re...
... brother was m...
... recovering from the ga...
My days are filled...

DENVER
NOV 3
8 1954
COLO.

3 CENTS 3   3 CENTS 3

VIA AIR MAIL

Mr. and Mrs. D.C. Hudkins
Kanopolis Lake
Marquette, Kansas

The rug — is ...
and we found it can
is cleaned. It will
bedroom. Your bro...
lovely, and I shall care

last week-end...
first recovering from the ga...

·EARLY DENVER·

"After New York, everyone here is so damn nice. I LIKE Denver,"

she wrote home to her mother.

When Dana left the ivy-covered halls of Radcliffe and returned home in the spring of 1954, she was a different person. At 23 and no longer a shy girl from a small town in Kansas, she had blossomed into an educated, charming woman, graceful and comfortable among advantaged and well-traveled people many years her senior. She was steady with a full martini glass—vodka only, preferably one olive—and had perfected her mother's smile to a wattage that was unforgettable. She was a popular dinner-party guest, relaxed and gracious and always ready with a story or a joke. Her presence at dinner tables, both as a guest and as a host, would become her hallmark.

She had devoured the book-learning dispensed by colleges, gained a taste of practical knowledge by interning in New York and Boston and allowed her natural interests to emerge. She was good at writing and enjoyed it, with a natural ability to find words that were crisp and persuasive—skills that would carry her into the fledgling field of public relations. She had an intuitive talent to present an issue, make compelling arguments and gently persuade readers toward her conclusions. She would develop these powers of persuasion into a fierce strength later in life.

(Cockwise from top left):
Skyline view of Denver, Cooper Post Card Company
Panoramic Aerial of Civic Center and Downtown Denver, Courtesy,
History Colorado (Postcard Collection), 92.35.121
Metropole Hotel & Broadway Theatre, Courtesy, History Colorado
(Postcard Collection), 89.451.2123
Union Station, Courtesy, History Colorado (Postcard Collection)

In June 1954, she boarded a train back to Kansas, tired but proud of her accomplishments. She was anxious to see her family, to get back to summer days at the marina and to be with childhood friends again.

Her mother hoped she might settle down in Salina, or at least in Kansas, and had lined up a number of job openings or job contacts for her—all of them in the state.

But Dana's horizon had grown wider. She considered working in Kansas City or St. Louis. She even thought of returning to Boston, which she had fallen in love with, but knew it would be nearly impossible to move back without a job and a place to live, neither of which she had. She thought about Denver, which wasn't that far from Salina, and remembered fondly the Colorado mountains and her family's fishing trips to Gunnison.

While in Cambridge, she had dated a Denverite, Fritz Tossberg, who had moved back to Denver. She called Fritz, who said he would be happy to introduce her around if she decided to move to Denver.

She took the train to Denver, arriving at the end of September 1954. She rented a room in the Argonaut Hotel, which still stands on the corner of Grant Street and Colfax Avenue, across from the State Capitol. Two weeks later, she rented a small apartment two blocks away at 1309 Grant Street, #106.

She wasted little time getting to know the city and its citizens. Fritz invited her to a Republican Party event featuring President Dwight Eisenhower, Vice President Richard Nixon and singer Ethel Merman. Eisenhower frequently visited Denver, partly because his wife, Mamie Doud, had grown up at 750 Lafayette Street and her family still lived there. The President also loved to golf and fly fish in Colorado, particularly along the Fraser River below the Winter Park ski area.

Dana found a surprising number of her college friends and sorority sisters now lived in Denver, and they too were happy to expand her social network. They took her to Boulder for football games, to the mountains where she had trouble with the altitude and to the Denver Country Club for drinks and dinner. She liked going to the Denver Press Club, the nation's oldest press club, because it was a popular watering hole where she could mingle with journalists, public relations people, judges, lawyers and a few cops.

"After New York, I can't recover from the surprise that everyone here is so damn nice," she wrote in her first letter home to her mother. "I LIKE Denver."

She also wrote that Denver was more "citified" than she had imagined, that it reminded her in certain ways of Boston. Denver was still "intact as a Victorian city," after its boom during the mining days in the late 1800s. "But no one talks about its history," she wrote. "The West has a fabulous history, and we need to be thinking about that."

The seeds of historic preservation were germinating.

Denver Country Club

Her job interviews went well. She agreed with her interviewers at the Rippey ad agency that she was overqualified for what they needed. She met The Denver Post city editor, Willard Hazelbush, who liked her right away and offered to help her find something. The Denver Dry Goods offered her a job in retail, which she turned down. She also interviewed at several oil companies for office positions, which she didn't want, still hoping to find something in public relations. She received several offers for good jobs, but they wouldn't be available for a couple of months. She remained upbeat.

Finally, a month after arriving in Denver, she accepted an offer to work at the William Kostka Public Relations Agency, at 1666 California St. Her first assignment was the March of Dimes account, which required her to visit polio victims in local hospitals and write about them. The experience deeply affected her. She also was assigned to the Goodwill Industries account, which required her to write short scripts for comedian Bob Hope to record for radio ads.

The public relations field was a good fit. Much of her work involved preparing copy for ads, giving tips to reporters or writing feature stories herself. She delivered them in person to The Denver Post and the Rocky Mountain News, where she developed first-name relationships with reporters and editors.

"The newspaper business is totally fascinating and fast moving, sometimes ruthless," she wrote home to her mother.

She wrote a delightful feature story for The Denver Post, replete with five of her photographs of young boys attending the Chief Ouray YMCA summer camp outside of Granby. The Post displayed the half-page story and photos, but omitted her byline, which was customary for stories from public relations people.

Denver Press Club, (left) dining room with member caricatures (right) fireplace lounge and bar

Photos: Dick Nosbisch

One important client of the Kostka Agency was the Convention and Visitors Bureau, which was promoting a new, 700-room hotel to be built at 16th Street and Court Place in the heart of downtown Denver. The hotel was the brainchild of William Zeckendorf, a brash, blustery New York real estate developer who stormed into Denver and began buying up prime real estate. Denver's wealthiest families had controlled most of the banking and development in the city for decades and suddenly, there was alarm, on the squash courts and in the men's grilles, that an "outsider", an "easterner" and a "Jewish realtor" could come into town and tell the natives how to develop their city.

It is difficult to gauge the depth of anti-Semitism in Denver at the time, but it was not impossible in mid-century Denver to hear a reference to the city's Hilltop neighborhood as "Kikes Peak."

WILLIAM ZECKENDORF

William Zeckendorf was a third-generation developer, the P.T. Barnum of real estate who could sell you the Brooklyn Bridge, then buy it back at a profit. He purchased Manhattan's decrepit slaughterhouses along the East River, sold the land for a $2 million profit to the Rockefeller family, which donated the site to the United Nations for its new world headquarters. Zeckendorf was fearless and unrelenting as a negotiator, and eventually gained control of the iconic Chrysler Building.

He was better than anyone at finding new uses for land that had been ignored or rundown. He bought an old horse barn and riding academy on the west side of Central Park and developed it into the headquarters of the fledgling American Broadcasting Co. (ABC). He bought a mile of Hoboken, N.J.'s rundown waterfront and shipping piers, cleaned them up and doubled his money within the year.

He joined the property management firm of Webb & Knapp, worked his way up to majority stockholder, then took it public in 1952.

He hated suburbs, which he called "parasites" on the core cities they surrounded, arguing they would never survive without a thriving core city. By 1960, he was the country's largest developer of urban residential housing, including the more than 260-acre Century City in Los Angeles. He cleared out numerous slums in New York, Chicago and Washington, D.C., and replaced them with middle-income housing.

He eventually acquired 9 hotels in Manhattan totaling 7,000 rooms, including the Plaza, the Astor, the Drake and others. His dream of building the largest hotel in the world continued to escape him, as did his plans to build the tallest office building in the country as well as the largest office building in the country by square footage, which at the time was the Pentagon.

Zeckendorf had deep pockets of cash, both his own and investors', and he was looking for places to spend it. Denver was ripe for development, Zeckendorf said, because it had no buildings taller than 12 stories and nothing of any significance had been built in the past 30 years. The city was being run by 20 wealthy families "knitted together through intermarriage" whose "country-club thinking" had done nothing to grow Denver since World War II, he said.

The Convention and Visitors Bureau, whose job was to promote economic growth, was happy to court Zeckendorf and his plans. But the locals' animosity toward him would become nastier than anything the bureau wanted to handle. So it hired the Kostka Agency to help sway public opinion about "Big Bill" Zeckendorf. Dana, by now Kostka's rising public relations star, was tapped for the nearly impossible job of convincing Denver that Zeckendorf would be a good neighbor.

Denver originally had been the county seat of the enormous Arapahoe County, which stretched 30 miles north-south and extended 175 miles east to Kansas. A lovely, but monstrously large, courthouse was built on the corner of 16th Street and Court Place in the late 1800s. In 1902, Denver voted to become a separate county. About the same time, the legislature created Adams County, which built its own courthouse to the north of Denver, and shrunk Arapahoe County, which built its own courthouse in Littleton. The grand and now abandoned courthouse in Denver was demolished in 1934, leaving a six-acre empty field. It sat fallow for about 20 years until Zeckendorf bought it in 1949, creating a furor among Denver's "garden clubs," as he called them. Sensing real development opportunities downtown, Zeckendorf went on a buying spree by purchasing the Paramount Theatre and the Kittredge Building near 16th and Glenarm streets, and other properties on Stout Street.

The Arapahoe County Courthouse between 15 and 16th streets on Court Place. Denver originally was part of Arapahoe County, which extended clear to Kansas. Denver became its own county in 1902. The courthouse was demolished in 1934.

Once Denver realized that Zeckendorf was serious about redeveloping a significant portion of the central business district, some business leaders tried to join him.

Claude Boettcher, scion of one of the 20 wealthy families ridiculed by Zeckendorf and whose family home is now the Governor's Mansion at 8th Ave. and Logan Street, flew to New York to meet Zeckendorf and propose a partnership to develop Court House Square. Zeckendorf was impressed by Boettcher and agreed to take him on as a partner.

The Denver Post dubbed Zekendorf "Parking Lot Bill"

Boettcher proposed a trial run by first developing a small parcel he owned on the northeast corner of 17th Avenue and Broadway, across from the Brown Palace Hotel. Zeckendorf agreed and brought in a young architect, Ieoh Ming Pei, who designed a 24-story "skyscraper" office building to be constructed with a steel skeleton. Boettcher, who

Denver Public Library, Western History Collection, X-23379

The parking lots created when the Arapahoe County Courthouse was demolished. New York developer William Zeckendorf built a department store and a 700-room hotel on the site. His workers allegedly found a gold nugget while digging the foundation, which Zeckendorf's wife made into cufflinks for him. The Sheraton Hotel occupies the site today.

owned Ideal Cement Co. and considered himself the de facto leader of the cement industry, was shocked when he learned it would not be built of concrete, and told Zeckendorf he would have to pull out because he could never develop a building made only of steel. Zeckendorf bought him out and built Denver's tallest building at the time, The Mile High Center, which opened in July 1955.

Meanwhile, Zeckendorf, busy with other projects, paved over the empty land at Court House Square and made it a parking lot, which brought him $80,000 in annual rent, one-tenth of what he had paid for it. The Denver Post dubbed him "Parking Lot Bill" and implored him to do something with the land.

Zeckendorf now was ready to develop Court House Square. He wanted a large hotel and a major department store on the property. To that end, he maneuvered Conrad Hilton to lease and operate a 700-room hotel there. He then bought the upscale but struggling Daniels and Fisher department store and planned to move it up 16th Street to the new complex. The May Company, another Denver department store which got its start in Leadville in the 1800s selling dungarees to miners, now was fearful of D&F's new prominence downtown, so May offered to buy D&F from Zeckendorf. The developer agreed to sell provided that the combined retail venture would lease his new building across from the new Hilton Hotel.

The package was complete and construction would soon begin. This was big news for Denver, and Zeckendorf flew out from New York on his own DC-3, along with his architect I.M.Pei, to make the announcement.

The Daniels & Fisher department store, which merged with the May Co. and moved to 16th and Court Place. The five-story department store was demolished but the clock tower was saved, and still stands at 16th and Arapahoe streets.

Dana, who had been handling much of the publicity for the project, drove out to Denver's new Stapleton Airport to pick up the two men. "They didn't get in until 10:30 that night," she said. "Both Zeckendorf and Pei had been drinking champagne the entire flight and were looped when they got off the plane. I got them into the car and drove to a press conference downtown.

"Zeckendorf sat at a desk to announce his project, grabbed a letter opener and began stabbing the desk for emphasis on every point he made. Pei and I were in the back of the room laughing at the bruising business presentation Big Bill was giving late in the night to room full of reporters."

"Big Bill" Zeckendorf's young architect, I.M. Pei, designed the hyperbolic paraboloid roof for the entrance into the new May D&F department store. An ice-skating rink was built in the open space to the left and named Zeckendorf Plaza. The Hilton Hotel is in the background, with 16th Street running to the left in the photo.

Around that same time, Zeckendorf let it be known they had found gold on the property, which caused a furor among the newspapers. Mayor Quigg Newton rushed in, insisting that the gold belonged to the City of Denver. Nobody seemed to know exactly where it had been found on the site. And no one questioned the irony of gold being found on a piece of land that had sat empty for 30 years then paved over six years earlier as a parking lot. Dana, rolling her eyes skyward, said it might have been found during the soil tests prior to digging the foundations. "All I know is how glad they (Zeckendorf's crew) were when they found gold," she said. "You know how the press is. They love stuff like that."

In his autobiography, Zeckendorf claimed they found only a tiny amount of gold, about $50,000 worth, and that he was given a small nugget which his wife turned into cufflinks for him.

Excavation of the former courthouse site began in 1956. About 60 feet down, the workers found an underground stream flowing through sand and gravel. Zeckendorf told them to keep digging, that the sand and gravel could be used for constructing the new buildings at a huge savings. Hence, the building has one of the deepest parking lots in downtown.

Construction underway for the new May D&F store and the Hilton Hotel. When the excavating crew allegedly struck gold, Mayor Quigg Newton insisted it belonged to the city. A fight ensued, with the daily newspapers reporting every move.

Shortly after she began working, Dana moved out of her Grant Street apartment and joined three other young women in a small, two-bedroom house at 135 Jackson Street, which she considered "rather far out" from downtown. A few blocks down the 1st Avenue hill, another developer, Temple Buell, had purchased a former landfill and was turning it into a retail shopping center, to be named for nearby Cherry Creek.

Dana's social life began to soar, whether it was the Black Sheeps Ball at the Denver Country Club, post-football game parties at the University of Colorado in Boulder, or "endless" martinis with boss Bill Kostka and co-workers every Friday in the Brown Palace Hotel.

Her new friend, Bunny Lazier, invited her to the annual Gridiron Dinner, put on by newspaper people at the Cosmopolitan Hotel, where she was seated with the presidents of both the Colorado Bar Association and the Denver Bar Association. She remarked that she met candidates for the U.S. House of Representatives and Senate, "who quickly lost interest in me when they learned I hadn't been in Denver long enough to register to vote."

By now it was nearly ski season, so she enrolled in dry-land training classes and soon was headed to Arapahoe Basin for her first runs.

After taking her share of tumbles down the bunny slopes one Saturday, she went in for hot chocolate, where she talked with "a dateless man", Jack Lamb, who agreed to meet her in the Alpine Bar—"a quaint little spot with a huge fireplace and comfy couches.

We drank a few hot buttered rums and I began to feel like an old hand on the slopes. This skiing is just great! The lingo is a scream!" she wrote home to her mother.

Back in Denver, Dana and her three roommates threw a martini party for 60 people in their tiny 2-bedroom house. It was the beginning of a skill she would hone for the rest of her life: gathering too many people for too many drinks resulting in hilarious laughter and making many new friends.

She took the train back to Salina for her first Christmas while living in Denver, driven to Union Station by her new friend Jack Lamb. She and Lamb grew quite fond of each other and continued dating and skiing together until he was abruptly reassigned to Salt Lake City. "So, our little tea party has ended," was how she summed up his departure.

She began skiing regularly, thoroughly enjoying it and improving her style and technique. Aspen, which had opened only a few years earlier, became her favorite destination, which she and her new friend, realtor Katie Billings, tried to visit as often as possible. Before construction of Interstate 70 in the '60s and '70s, Aspen was a six-hour drive on a two-lane road and it would take them until midnight on a Friday to arrive from Denver.

They'd drive directly to famed ski racer Steve Knowlton's new hot spot, the Golden Horn. Knowlton, a member of the first U.S. Olympic ski teams in the late 1940s, was a gregarious, handsome guy with a wide smile and a quick laugh, perfect for being the front-man in the series of nightclubs he would own. Eventually, he moved to Denver where he owned The Buckhorn Exchange on Osage Street, the oldest restaurant in Denver, with liquor license #1. He was later executive director of Ski Country USA, with offices in Larimer Square.

Soon Dana tired of four women sharing a two-bedroom apartment so she moved with her cousin into a one-bedroom, basement apartment at 615 Clayton Street, near Congress Park. Money was tight because of so much skiing and partying, but she still had her priorities. Somehow, she managed to scrape together enough to buy a new pair of lace-up ski boots for a whopping $28.50.

Dana was fun and delightful to be with. She had no trouble attracting men. She was glamorous, well-educated, energetic and full of adventure. Her dance card was always full. She knew very well how much she had to offer. She set her standards high, as her mother had taught her, and she could be very picky with suitors. She continued to work on the Convention and Visitors Bureau account, and even began dating some of Zeckendorf's men.

Despite a full social calendar and many suitors, Dana fell quickly for a young geologist, John Crawford, a daredevil skier with "great legs".

Shortly after she got her new apartment, in the spring of 1955, she wrote to her mother that she was dating quite a lot. "You have no idea how hectic my life is. Not so hectic as full. I am dating too many different people. Just to give you an idea, here are the main people who are feeding, drinking and entertaining me occasionally":

Dave XXXX *(from a very prominent Denver family)*—**"lawyer, Annapolis and Yale Law School-tall-handsome-bright-skier-DULL."**

Bob XXXX—**"lawyer, Cornell graduate making a killing in oil and uranium promotion-skier-conceited but entertaining."**

Frank XXXX—**"too old and set in his ways."**

Bill XXXX—**"Harvard grad from Concord, Mass. Making great progress with the Great Western Sugar Co.-good cook. Rather difficult to talk to at times."**

Dave XXXX—**"CU grad, lives in Boulder, in real estate biz—ex-ski instructor in Aspen. Is helping me with my skiing—dear boy—cleans rugs on the side." (She then draws a light bulb with the caption "IDEA!")**

Jim XXXX—**"for cocktails and lunch and coffee."**

"It sounds pretty gay but it ain't. The brightest spot is skiing. I'd rather do that than eat," she wrote. And based on her finances, she wasn't buying much food because she was skiing every weekend, in either Winter Park or Aspen.

Roughly a month after she inventoried her dance card for her mother, she made first mention of a young man, John Crawford—"An outstanding, charming geologist for a wealthy oil firm," who took her to a cocktail party at the Denver Country Club. Perhaps trying to prepare her mother for a relationship that seemed to be going smoother and faster than the others, she referred to Crawford in a letter as "an old friend," a phrase triggered perhaps by the fact that he was 10 years older than Dana. Years later, she recalled that she had fallen in love observing him at a party. "I fell in love with his legs. He had great legs. I have always been a leg person."

She and Crawford went with two other couples to the Broadmoor Hotel for May Day weekend—"a wonderful weekend, swimming, visiting the zoo, steaks and martinis. Expect to hear more about Crawford, but he's only a friend—a buddy pact," she told her mother. She also mentioned that Crawford loved the outdoors, loved to fish and loved to camp. "Could you send me a sleeping bag from home?" she closed her letter.

As spring warmed into summer, she grew bored with her job, although she enjoyed putting out the first edition of the new magazine, "Denver Young Men."

She had several dates with Bill Nicholson, son of Denver's new mayor, Will Nicholson, but admitted in a letter to her mother that she was waiting for John Crawford to return from a field trip in two weeks. After a July 4 weekend trip with Crawford to Lake of the Ozarks in Missouri, they had dinner—prime rib and martinis (olive)—at the Ship Tavern in the Brown Palace Hotel. In a letter to her mother, this beau had no warts—"John Crawford…A GOOD MAN," she wrote.

By the end of the summer of 1955, Dana and John, both solid in their mutual admiration, made a spur-of-the-moment trip to Salina to meet her parents for the first time. John later wrote an apologetic letter to Dana's father saying he had hoped to talk with him about proposing to his daughter but found the circumstances too difficult.

John had been married once before, briefly, and had been unhappy. This one would turn out differently. He adored Dana and the two shared many interests beyond skiing and socializing. The couple was married on Oct. 12, 1955 in Tulsa, John's hometown, because John's mother, Muriel, had been in a serious accident and was unable to travel. John's father had passed away before John and Dana met.

"John Crawford…A GOOD MAN"

John Williams Roy Crawford III as a soldier in World War II, serving under Gen. George S. Patton in the Third Army's drive across France and into Nazi Germany.

John Williams Roy Crawford III as a student at the Colorado School of Mines.

Political cartoonist, Thomas Nast.

John Crawford III's great-grandfather was Thomas Nast, the political cartoonist best known for bringing down Boss Tweed and his Tammany Hall political machine in New York City in the 1860s. His cartoons were the first to use an elephant as the symbol of the Republican Party. His illustrations of Clement Moore's poem "'Twas the Night Before Christmas," are said to be the original images of our modern-day Santa Claus in the red suit and white beard. Dana has a half-dozen original Nast prints hanging in the front hallway of her loft.

Nast's cartoons brought him celebrity status and he traveled extensively across the country. In Colorado, there is the 12,454-foot Mt. Nast in Pitkin County, roughly halfway between Leadville and Aspen. Nast allegedly invested in the Colorado Midland Railway, which came up out of Leadville west over Hagerman Pass near the soon-to-be-named Mt. Nast.

One of Nast's daughters married John Williams Roy Crawford, a handsome, well liked man who worked his way up to become William Rockefeller's partner for a short while. William and brother John D. Rockefeller were co-founders of the Standard Oil Co.

John W.R. Crawford II moved from New York to Oklahoma, where he struggled as a wildcatter, drilling a number of dry holes before finally striking oil. He had three sons: John III, the oldest; Peter Roy Crawford, who became a landman in the oil industry; and David Roy Crawford, an architect who lived with his family in Atlanta.

John Crawford III, born in 1922, grew up in Tulsa and after graduating from Phillips Academy in Massachusetts in 1941 enrolled in the Colorado School of Mines in Golden, where he studied petroleum engineering. He quit his studies to fight in World War II, serving under Gen. George A. Patton in his Third Army, which played a key role in the Battle of the Bulge.

Duke Crawford, Dana and John's youngest son, recalled his father as a very sweet man, very giving and almost overly sensitive. "My father lived through that (WWII). He was a sergeant with illiterate kids in his unit, from the south. He would read them their letters from home, then help them write letters back to their families," Duke recalled. "Then some would die."

The newlyweds took a one-week honeymoon and drove to Taos, N.M., which Dana called "a heavenly, sleepy place" where she threatened to stay and become an artist. Upon their return to the basement apartment at 615 Clayton St., John resumed his hectic traveling schedule. The two began skiing constantly, with Dana so happy that she had found "a ski instructor for life."

"He was a daredevil skier," recalled Tom Congdon, a close friend of John and Dana, who owned a house in Aspen. "I remember him standing at the top of Aspen Mountain, tucking down and skiing straight down. I couldn't keep up with him. He was a real risky skier, and a good story teller. He was a lot of fun after a day of skiing."

John's work as an up-and-coming geologist for Argo Oil was going very well and he won several promotions. Argo was expanding rapidly into Canada and John was promoted to head the company's geology department. His income was large enough to allow Dana to quit the Kostka agency and concentrate on making a home for the couple, although it was still a cramped, one-bedroom basement apartment.

As a new bride, this would be Dana's first Christmas away from her parents. She planned for it thoroughly, scrubbing the apartment spotless, opening and polishing all their wedding presents. She and John hand-made 200 Christmas cards, which they signed and mailed off to family and friends. Dana was happy, consulting with her mother over the long-distance phone line about her favorite recipes and table settings.

To celebrate the close of their momentous year, the Crawfords joined a group of 15 others and rented an 8-bedroom house in Aspen for two weeks over New Year's. With the legs and stamina of 20-somethings, they skied every day until the lifts closed. From there, it was après-ski drinks at the Jerome Hotel, followed by full dinners at any one of the new restaurants springing up in this charming, former silver-mining town. Nightcaps always were at Steve Knowlton's Golden Horn nightclub before sliding into warm beds to recharge for another day of the same.

Soon after returning from Aspen, 24-year-old Dana announced to her parents that she was pregnant with her first child. The baby wasn't due until July, which made the math add up perfectly for her mother's approval. Their whirlwind social life continued unabated through the winter, although Dana began to cut back on skiing.

In early 1956, the Crawfords purchased their first house together at 629 Humboldt Street, a solid, two-story home in a fashionable, leafy neighborhood north of the Denver Country Club. It had been the home of Ken Perry, founder of Bishop-Perry Real Estate, who moved into his mother's home on Circle Drive. After much painting and refurbishing, the couple moved in that April. In true Crawford fashion, they threw a house-warming cocktail party for 30 people, which Dana mused "went way too late."

John launched himself into the garden, which had been neglected somewhat, and planted everything he could find, from roses to irises to blackberry bushes. Gardening and yard work had always been a favorite pastime for him and would continue to be so for the rest of his life.

Dana had made a name for herself handling the Zeckendorf project and began receiving job offers, including one to run the office of a prosperous oil and uranium mining firm for a hefty salary of $350 per month. But she turned them down.

Instead, she left her job at the Kostka agency shortly after her wedding and picked up several PR clients of her own, managing them out of a small office in her new home. She was settling into her new life quite comfortably, handling the housework including washing clothes in the "Bendix" and raising a pitch-black puppy which she named "Pirate."

Courtesy, Crawford Collection

Dana in the yard of her parents' house in Salina, Kansas, with her four young boys, Jack, Tom, Peter and Duke, in chronological order. The four were born within five years, with three of them in diapers at any one time. At the same time, she began making plans for developing Larimer Square.

John Williams Roy Crawford IV (Jack) arrived on June 8, 1956, slightly, but not suspiciously, ahead of schedule, healthy and energetic.

Dana adapted easily to the new priorities of a crying baby, midnight feedings, diapers and bathing. She and her husband continued their social vortex with dinner parties, the theater, opera in Central City, CU football games and ski trips to Aspen and Winter Park, sometimes riding the Rio Grande Ski Train.

Dana thrived in her new roles as wife and mother. She and John got right to work growing their family: Tom arrived 12 months after Jack, on June 25, 1957; Peter arrived on October 17, 1958; and Duke on October 8, 1960. She had four boys on the ground before she and John celebrated their 5th anniversary.

"I had three boys in diapers at one time," she joked. "They were just wild, high energy and fought with one another, Duke and Tom especially."

Dana continued with the few private PR accounts she had acquired and took on more work counseling moderately troubled students at nearby Morey Middle School. kShe also graded papers for 25 cents each. "I'd do laundry and grade papers at night. It was a lot of work, before the days of disposable diapers."

John was traveling a lot, which Dana said simplified things. His mother, still somewhat incapacitated from the accident and walking with a brace, came to visit frequently from Tulsa. "She liked staying at the Brown Palace," said Dana. "I'd have to pick her up, take her to lunch, then back to the hotel. I could manage two generations very well…the third was difficult."

LARIMER STREET

No 734. LARIMER ST: from 15th ST: DENVER. COLO.

Larimer street looking south from 15th Street around the turn of the century. Denver's original City Hall can be seen in the distance. The bell from the towering belfry is permanently mounted in a historical display at the corner of 14th and Larimer streets

"My mother said I should appear in the newspapers only three times...birth, marriage and death. Larimer Square turned into a project with a huge amount of press. My mother never would have approved."

Dana's first 10 years in Denver gave her the sense of stability and permanence she had grown up with in Salina. She had married well to John Crawford and the two of them now were establishing their family of four young boys, all high energy, rambunctious and feisty. They had a small house in an old section of town, a neighborhood of young families, older empty nesters and grassy parks within walking distance.

Dana distinguished herself at work, and actually outgrew her duties. As her family grew, she quit her job to stay at home with the boys. John's work was challenging and rewarding, so the family was financially comfortable. John was forced to travel extensively, which allowed Dana some time alone.

These quiet interludes gave her the opportunity to reflect on those early influences in her life — comfortable places where families and friends would gather, and the town squares, plazas and meeting places which she felt were so important for communities. She started paying more attention to how people gathered and socialized, particularly in public.

"From the day I arrived in Denver, I realized that a place was so badly needed where people from all backgrounds could get together and celebrate the city," she said.

Dana's small-town childhood was the foundation of this reverie. Residents of towns like Salina knew each other, talked freely, played together and shared their lives.

During her time at Dana Farm, she came to love the small, near-by town of Marietta, Ohio, with its New England-styled town square, park benches and pathways designed for pedestrians, and stores that catered to shoppers on foot. "Marietta was very charming, with a lovely downtown. It was very New Englandy. It made an impression on me, part of what was shaping me."

Her college years were spent on idyllic campuses: Monticello, across the river from St. Louis, with its elegant and stately Victorian architecture; the University of Kansas in Lawrence, an historic, tree-lined campus of peacefulness and purpose; and the ivy-covered halls of Radcliffe in Cambridge, Mass.

"Every school I attended had an influence on me, and particularly the towns around Boston," she said.

In Cambridge, she began to appreciate the older architecture, the brick sidewalks and walls, with footpaths leading over to Harvard Square or down to the banks of the Charles River. She loved traveling around New England, visiting villages and towns that had been laid out before the automobile era. Nearly every village had as its center the town square or plaza, where people gathered to hear news from town criers or gossip from friends and neighbors. Citizens also met there in celebration and protest. In these town centers, merchants peddled fish, meat and produce alongside the inns, pubs and bars for socializing.

"New England was filled with places for people to get out onto the streets," she said.

By the time Dana settled in Colorado, she knew what brought citizens together in communities and found examples in mountain towns like Georgetown, Idaho Springs, Empire and Fraser. But it was the gritty little village of Aspen that really captured her imagination, with its metamorphosis from a scruffy silver-mining camp into a cosmopolitan community of Bauhaus architecture, modern art and gatherings of intellectual luminaries such as Albert Schweitzer, Thornton Wilder and Arthur Rubinstein.

Early Aspen, where Chairlift #1, the longest in the world, opened on Jan. 1, 1947. Through the efforts of Walter Paepcke, Fritz Benedict and others, Aspen preserved much of its silver-mining heritage and became a big influence on Dana's ideas for preservation

"I started going to Aspen all the time, mainly to ski and to party" she said. "I loved that town, with Walter Paepcke and his Aspen Institute and all that was going on. (Architect) Fritz Benedict had started working and the town was already putting in some design controls. Master-planned communities were just starting."

"Place-making hadn't really developed yet as a widely known urban goal."

ASPEN

Aspen started in the late 1800s as a very productive mining town, with silver veins so rich they were visible in the rocks. The Smuggler Mine, on the north edge of town, produced a hefty portion of the world's supply of silver, including the largest silver nugget ever found in the world to this day---1,840 pounds.

The town had fallen on hard times during the Depression and World War II, covered in grime from coal stoves and dusty roads. But the Roaring Fork River valley was gorgeous, with terrific trout fishing and elk hunting, and soon war vets were returning to where the 10th Mountain Division had trained for combat.

Elizabeth "Pussy" Paepcke, wife of Chicago industrialist Walter Paepcke, allegedly climbed one side of Aspen Mountain with three girlfriends and skied down into town. Her enthusiasm for the valley convinced her husband to visit in the summer of 1946, and shortly after he founded and funded the Aspen Institute, which remains a leading cultural and artistic organization today. Paepcke, who had been a major supporter of the Bauhaus movement in the United States, invited friends to Aspen, including artist/architect Herbert Bayer, who had studied in Germany with Bauhaus founder Walter Gropius. Word spread quickly about the pleasures of summertime Aspen.

Soon, national ski champion Dick Durrance proposed a ski area, and, with the help of Denver heiress Ruth Humphreys Brown who donated $5,000, the Aspen Mountain ski area was opened to the public in January 1947, with the longest chairlift in the world. Durrance thanked Brown by naming the ever-popular "Ruthie's Run" after her. Ski racers from around the world competed in the 1951 FIS World Championships there, putting Aspen on the map in the wintertime as well.

She later contrasted that with Vail, which was being built in 1961-62 as a ski resort with no other focus. "Vail was a place in search of a spirit," Dana said. "What would it be without skiing?"

Dana's notion of urban revitalization centered on people and their times spent together. This highly social woman wanted a gathering spot for people, where they could eat, drink and mingle. She appreciated older structures she could renovate. But she hadn't yet developed her penchant for historic preservation.

Though still very young, she had been tutored in the rudiments of commercial real estate, mostly because of her PR work with Bill Zeckendorf and his dealings with City Hall and the city's wealthier families. Still, she had never built anything on her own and, in fact, never owned a piece of real estate except the house she and her husband bought. But her vision was becoming clearer and her enthusiasm followed.

In 1963 Dana was asked to chair a large fund-raising event at the University Hills shopping center on behalf of the Junior League. It was patterned after the Parisian flea markets, with many booths and various carnival rides and games. The event was scheduled over the Labor Day holiday and would need a significant number of Junior League volunteers. That would take all of Dana's powers of persuasion to convince these stylish women to abandon their weekend vacation plans in favor of working with her at the fundraiser.

In the midst of all of this activity, life struck a tragic blow to Dana. Dana's mother, Jo, dropped dead of a heart attack on June 10, 1963. There had been no warning, no signs of weakness or poor health. She had been vacationing in Arizona for a month when she returned, tan and full of life, to her home in Salina and dropped dead at the age of 55. Dana was about to turn 32.

Jo had been Dana's bedrock since birth. She was Dana's closest friend, her confidante, her mentor, her go-to person for anything, throughout Dana's life. The two had remained uncommonly close, even for mother and daughter, and had mailed each other handwritten letters at least every other week for the 15 years since Dana left home for college. Their letters were sweet, supportive, confessional at times and loving. Dana had such an easy flow with her mother, happily asking for advice or recipes, proudly boasting of her accomplishments in her new home, her jobs, her skiing, and now her new husband and four sons, whom Jo had been out to visit numerous times.

Courtesy, Crawford Collection

The last photo of Dana's mother, Josephine Dana Hudkins, taken one month before she died suddenly in June 1963 of a heart attack when she was 55, She and Dana were very close and had written letters to each other on an average of every two weeks since Dana had left for college 20 years earlier. She never got to see Larimer Square.

John and the four boys were equally devastated.

Dana still had her father, who always had been loving and supportive. But he wasn't nearly as demonstrative as her mother, and certainly wasn't as close to Dana as Jo was. Dale Hudkins wasn't critical of his only child. It's just that his approvals weren't readily handed out; they came infrequently, and that was difficult for Dana. He would remain in Salina for the rest of his life, living alone, with his marina and golfing friends to occupy his time, until his death 22 years later.

After returning from the memorial services in Salina, Dana took a long while to recover. Gradually, her attitude warmed, her enthusiasm returned and her vision came back into focus. She continued to organize and plan what would become the Junior League's most successful fundraising event to date, raising some $35,000 for its charitable fund. The experience of organizing such a large flea market and coordinating it with the shopping mall's management during a busy holiday weekend proved to be perfect for Dana's future role of running Larimer Square. She learned how shopping centers work. And that success reinforced her determination to continue with her plans for the future.

"By now, I had talked so much about doing this (Larimer Square) that I had to do it," she said.

Armed only with that vision and an old car, Dana had no particular location in mind and began driving the city, imagining what buildings might work and what wouldn't. She visited a number of buildings on a small hill on the northeastern edge of downtown, near the intersection of 20th Avenue and Lincoln Street, where the old Exodus nightclub hosted local singer Judy Collins, and groups like Peter, Paul and Mary and the Kingston Trio.

She looked at the 6-story Elkhorn Hotel nearby, which was owned by the Shafroth family. She also looked around the Cosmopolitan Hotel near 17th Avenue and Broadway, and at the Savoy Hotel.

She drove down near the South Platte River, along Boulder Street, under the 15th Street viaduct where My Brother's Bar grills its popular hamburgers and where REI later took over the enormous red-brick generating plant for Denver's trolley system and converted it into one of its flagship stores for outdoor gear and clothing.

She drove throughout downtown Denver, through the newer sections and through the older sections, places that proper women normally didn't visit. She spent so much time scouting locations that the locals began to notice her.

"I drove a puke green convertible. I drove it down there and it vapor locked. (Cars back then would overheat in Colorado's altitude until the gas line got so hot the liquid gas would turn to vapor and the engine would die). The bums knew how to fix it and helped me get it going."

She made friends with the Larimer Street beat cop, Swede Schalbrack, who kept an eye out for her as he kept the peace along Denver's skid row. Swede was quick with his nightstick and kept the peace in his own style.

"He said when the bouncers in the bum bars tossed a troublemaker out of a bar onto the street, he'd throw the guy back into the bar and keep him off the street."

Larimer Street in 1963 was a tough place, considered the backbone of Denver's Skid Row. You'd pass a pawn shop, a loan shop, cheap bars and liquor stores specializing in single cans of beer and two-ounce "nips" of hard liquor. Doorways, inset from the sidewalks' flow of traffic, collected wind-blown pages of newspapers and broken vodka bottles. Most reeked of urine and many were occupied by curled up, lifeless lumps of drunk men in filthy and torn clothes.

The west side of the 1400 block of Larimer Street as Dana found it in 1963. Above, her Ford convertible, which the bums on Skid Row would fix when it vapor locked.

Courtesy, Crawford Collection

But one day, she turned her convertible down Larimer Street and noticed how quaint and unique the 1400 block was, with attractive architecture on both sides of the street. It was early 1964.

She had driven this block many times before, unremarkably. But on this trip, the architecture jumped out at her, and the fact that the buildings were mostly intact. Curious, she drove to the Denver Public Library to investigate the block and its history. She learned that it was one of the most historically important blocks in the entire city.

"That was my 'Eureka' moment. This block was a huge slice of the very start of the city," she recalled. "I get lots of ideas. Some happen, some don't. But this idea was the hand of fate."

She learned that Denver, for all practical purposes, had started on the 1400 block of Larimer Street. It was filled with "firsts": General William Larimer, for whom the street would be named, in 1858 built the first house in Denver, a 16x20-foot log cabin, on the southeast corner of 15th and Larimer, where the Granite Building now stands. The block had been home to Denver's first post office, the first barber shop and allegedly Denver's first cat house. Across 14th Street was the site of Denver's first City Hall, which was torn down in the 1940s. The bronze bell from its cupola still remains there as a memorial.

Dana and two unidentified colleagues admire the bell from Denver's original City Hall, permanently mounted on display at 14th and Larimer streets

THE FOUNDING OF DENVER AND AURARIA

As Gen. Larimer built his first house in the village originally known as St. Charles, other settlers, mostly gold prospectors, set up a rival encampment on the south side of Cherry Creek, which they named Auraria. The encampments were set up after the first flecks of gold had been found in Cherry Creek and in the South Platte River. Miners understood that gold flecks found in rivers had been washed or eroded off of veins of gold high in the mountains. As the rugged prospectors climbed higher into the mountains searching for veins, the less adventurous folks remained behind, many of them earning a fair living by supplying the miners with equipment and clothing. Auraria grew rapidly to 250 buildings, while St. Charles lagged behind with 150 buildings. But the St. Charles people convinced the first railroad to put a depot and loading docks in their town, which doomed Auraria's economy. Soon, Aurarians waded across the creek to join St. Charles, which would be renamed Denver City after James W. Denver, territorial governor of Kansas. The state of Colorado was incorporated 15 years later in 1876.

In the late 1800s, Larimer Street, from Cherry Creek to 18th Street, would become Denver's equivalent of Broadway—a bustling thoroughfare of commerce, legislation, schmoozing and socializing. The "boulevard" was anchored on the south by Denver's first City Hall, an imposing building with a four-story belfry, built in 1883. The thoroughfare was anchored on the north, five blocks up on 18th, by the elegant, five-story Windsor Hotel, built in 1880. On 16th was the stone, five-story Tabor Block (office building not to be confused with the Tabor Opera House on Curtis Street), where the legislature convened prior to the opening of the state capitol. Visitors to Denver arrived at Union Station, then sauntered four blocks up to some of the finest dining in the country in the Manhattan Restaurant at 1551 Larimer or in Delmonico of the West, considered to be one of the finest steak houses in the country. City Hall was torn down in the 1940s. The original bronze bell is mounted on a memorial at 14th and Larimer streets.

Excitedly, Dana told her husband about her discovery and plans for the block. He was happy for her, although slightly skeptical. "Dana," he said, "You'll always find a way to get into trouble. You might as well find a way to get into trouble while making money."

None of the existing 18 buildings were the original buildings because of a massive fire in 1863 that leveled the majority of wooden buildings in early Denver. But it was the only block in downtown Denver where almost every building had been built or rebuilt before 1900.

At last, her search was over. Her unfocused vision for "place-making" had taken her on a journey that finally ended in the 1400 block of Larimer Street. She had no second thoughts about her choice. Now was the time to see if she could gain control of the buildings and the block.

She started by making daily visits to the assessor's office, learning who owned which building, how much they were valued, how long ago they were purchased, for how much and what the taxes were on each.

Her first task was to assemble the properties—to buy them outright or, at the very least, convince holdout owners to lease their buildings to her.

"We tried from the very start to acquire all of the 18 buildings and manage them as a small shopping center," she said. "I decided to call it a square to separate it from the rest of the street, even though it's not a square. I wanted it to become a destination in people's minds as 'Larimer Square.'"

Dana had two role models for organizing the square: Ghirardelli Square in San Francisco, which was only a few months ahead of Dana's plan; and Gaslight Square in St. Louis, which had been rollicking for nearly 10 years.

She also was heavily influenced by the Country Club Plaza in Kansas City, Missouri, the oldest continuously operating shopping center in the world. The Plaza was created in 1923 by J.C. Nichols, a highly successful but controversial developer who was the first to use a percentage lease with rents based on a percentage of gross sales. The Plaza had no asphalt parking lots. Cars were parked below ground, or hidden on rooftops and behind stores.

It was designed with a heavy European and Spanish influence. "It was gorgeous," Dana said, "and very successful."

GHIRARDELLI SQUARE

Ghirardelli Square was unique in that the Ghirardelli family had owned the entire block since the late 1800s. The chocolate manufacturer was bought out in the early 1960s and its headquarters was moved across the bay to San Leandro. The William Roth family bought the property in 1962 to prevent it from being turned into expensive apartments. They hired an architect, who developed the property into a touristy mix of restaurants and curio shops. All were contained within the old chocolate factory. It opened officially on Nov. 29, 1964, just 13 months before Dana would officially open Larimer Square.

Dana visited Ghirardelli Square and met with its owners, who agreed to give her whatever advice they could. The biggest difference between the two projects was that Ghirardelli Square was owned entirely by one family and was wholly contained in the old factory. All shops and restaurants were tenants, not owners, which greatly simplified control of the enterprise.

GASLIGHT SQUARE

Gaslight Square in downtown St. Louis was very different. It had been built in the 1950s as an entertainment district mimicking the days of riverboats, gambling and honky-tonk music. Gas street lamps gave it its name.

Gaslight Square became enormously popular in the late 1950s and grew to an estimated 50 different businesses, mostly music and dance halls, restaurants, cafes and antique shops. In the 1960s, hippies and poets, like Jack Kerouac and Allen Ginsberg, passed through, soon to be followed by celebrity entertainers such as Barbra Streisand, Miles Davis, the Smothers Brothers and Woody Allen, who all performed there.

Time Magazine profiled Gaslight Square in February 1963, prompting Dana to visit there several times. Technically, it was an entertainment district with multiple buildings and multiple owners. Most adhered to the "riverboat" theme but some owners' styles, décor and atmosphere clashed.

Dana made friends with the owner of the Three Fountains Restaurant, who cautioned her to never underestimate how different and how competitive the various property and business owners could be.

From its peak in 1962, Gaslight Square began to deteriorate because there was no cohesive organization to keep things running cooperatively. By the late 1960s, it had declined to a shadow of its rowdy former self.

"In Gaslight Square, I learned what not to do," Dana said.

Two things became very clear to her. She had to purchase as much of the real estate in Larimer Square as she could, then gain control of the remainder through leases or partnerships. She also had to start raising money from investors not only to purchase the properties but to clean them up and get them rented.

The two biggest hurdles in buying or "assembling" a group of buildings is to convince all the owners to sell and not let them find out they're all selling to the same person. "If the owners learned somebody was coming in to buy everything, the buildings quickly become very pricey," she said.

So Dana began making up names for different purchasers, like the ABC Company or the XYZ Corporation. "No one knew they were all the same company," she said.

She asked real estate broker Harris Kelly to help approach the owners with her plans to buy them out. He was sworn to secrecy, and agreed. She also hired attorney Hardin Holmes, whom she had met at a party in Boulder. Holmes worked for the firm Ireland, Stapleton, Pryor and Pascoe and had assembled the land to build Brooks Tower three blocks away on 15th and Curtis streets. The elaborate Mining Exchange building had occupied that site until it was pushed over in Denver Urban Renewal Authority's hysteria to build new. The only thing saved was the bronze statue of the miner holding a nugget of gold that now sits in front of Brook Tower. It had been on the roof of the exchange building.

Colorado News Company

The grand Mining Exchange Building at 15th and Curtis streets, torn down in the early 1960s to make way for the Brooks Tower residential building. The 12-foot tall copper statue of a miner holding a gold nugget, seen on top of this photo, now stands near the sidewalk of 15th Street between Curtis and Arapahoe streets.

To convince investors to join her, she knew she couldn't parade each and every one of them down to Larimer Street to show them around. She decided they didn't need to see inside the dilapidated buildings, so she built a three-dimensional model of the block. She hired a prominent photographer, Laura Gilpin, who had photographically documented the rise of the Central City Opera, among other things.

Gilpin had the ability to photograph buildings square and true, without distorting them, which was a difficult trick. Dana paid her $600, with money she had found in her mother's desk.

"We came down on Sunday mornings when no one was around, always on Sundays, so no one would see us. This gal came down with ladders, props of trees and bushes, all sorts of things."

As the photographs arrived, Dana sat in her house, amid the rumble of four young boys, and carved small blocks of balsa wood into tiny, three-dimensional models of each building. For the fronts of the buildings, she cut up the photographs, which had to be absolutely straight and proportional, without any distortion, and glued them on the front of the balsa wood models. On a flat piece of hardboard about two feet wide by three feet long, she glued the models together in two rows, with the street and sidewalks in between.

"We made the model with little gaslights and cars. I pasted the cut-outs myself on the balsa," she said. "Curt Fentress' first wife made all the graphics."

She began making offers for the properties in 1964 and early 1965. Her first attempt to purchase a property was a gutsy choice, typical of Dana's style to dive right in. She walked into Colorado National Bank and approached Rike Wootten, the bank's assistant vice president and a former Marine pilot who held a Harvard MBA. Wootten owned three buildings on the east side of Larimer—The Sussex Hotel at 1428-1434, the Kettle Building at 1426, and what's known today as the Wootten Building at 1416-22 Larimer Street.

"Dana walked into my office and said, 'You don't know me but I have this idea of making a sort of fun shopping district on Larimer Street.' I asked her if she was sure of what she was doing? So she invited me over to her house 'to see some pictures I have glued together.'"

Wootten, who's had the same Marine Corps flattop haircut for 50 years, said he used to spend his lunch hours at the bank walking around downtown Denver. One of those walks took him down the 1400 block of Larimer Street, which he knew was considered Skid Row. On a whim, he bought three buildings "for nothing down and something owed," or about $50,000 for all three.

The Kettle Building was merely a shell with a front and a back that shared the sidewalls with the neighboring buildings. Bird droppings in the attic were six inches deep.

The Sussex Hotel had a unique architectural feature—a water-driven elevator. The alley to the east was about eight feet higher than Larimer Street, so the Sussex Building had a short elevator in it, powered by the city's pressurized water line. Deliveries made in the back were placed on the elevator, the operator pulled a rope and the cylinder drained out the water, lowering the elevator to the main floor level. The operator pulled another rope and water pressure pushed the cylinder and elevator back to the top. "It worked just fine. But it didn't last long in the remodel," Wootten said.

"The Sussex Hotel was the best flophouse in Denver. But the city shut it down a year after I bought it when a guy died in it and wasn't found for a week," Wootten said. "With no revenue coming in, I didn't know how to pay the mortgage."

Sussex Building before

Sussex Building after

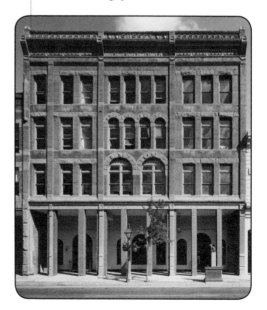

Dana's timing was perfect.

"I was about to tear them down because I didn't know what else to do," Wootten said. "I had talked with some bar owners from Aspen about selling it to them but that went nowhere. So I went along with Dana."

Wootten liked Dana's plans so much that he agreed to invest in the project. In exchange for half ownership of his three buildings, Wootten was given 6,250 shares of stock in Larimer Square Inc. Wootten then called his brother, John, a banker in their native Oklahoma, to invest a small amount as well.

Wootten blushed slightly when asked about the wisdom of investing with a woman with no real estate experience who was buying historical buildings when the national fever was to push them over. "My wife, Barbara, said, 'You're crazy.' She wasn't far wrong." (Barbara Stearns Wootten was the daughter of Robert Stearns, president of the University of Colorado as well as dean of its law school.)

About the same time, Tom Congdon, the Aspen skiing friend of Dana's and John's, stopped by the Crawford house in Denver one day and saw Dana's little model of Larimer Street.

"What's this?" he asked innocently.

Congdon, another Harvard MBA and who came from oil and mining wealth, had grown his family's fortune quite successfully. So Dana didn't hesitate to rope him into investing in Larimer Square, a decision he says he's never regretted, adding that 50 years later he still has money invested in her projects.

"I was intrigued, particularly with the idea of reusing old buildings," he said. "John and I were in our drinking days back then and we envisioned a string of saloons along both sides of Larimer Street."

Congdon convinced another friend, William Dorn Miller, head of Forest Oil, and his wife, Rhea, to invest as well.

With significant success so far in raising funds and attracting investors, Dana approached one of Denver's best-known society members, Richard "Dick" Gibson, who worked for the investment firm, Boettcher and Co. He also was an original investor in the hugely popular Water Pik dental device. But he was best known for his Labor Day Jazz Parties, which he held in Denver or Aspen or Vail or wherever he could gather some 500 of his closest friends for 3 days of music, friendship, dining and drinking.

Denver Public Library, Western History Collection,
Rocky Mountain News, May 23, 1965

Dana explains architectural renderings of Larimer Square to Denver Mayor Tom Currigan, center, and investor Rike D. Wootten, seven months before the square opened.

Over the course of 30 years, the jazz became so good that some of the top musicians in the country joined in—saxophonist Zoot Sims, trumpeter Yank Lawson, guitarist Johnny Smith, pianist Ralph Sutton and Benny Goodman's trombonist Cutty Cutshall—and soon they were known as "The World's Greatest Jazz Band." Jazz critic Whitney Balliett attended the 1969 party at Aspen's Hotel Jerome and Red Onion nightclub and wrote a definitive jazz piece, "Ecstasy At The Onion," for The New Yorker magazine.

On May 27, 1964, Dana handed Gibson a two-paragraph letter describing her vision for Larimer Square:

"In an authentic setting on the most famous street in Denver, Larimer Square will bring new flavor to this well known city at the foot of the Rockies…It will recapture the gaiety and excitement of the early days with all Larimer Square buildings dating in the 1860s and 1870s."

"Larimer Square will transform a shabby district into a handsome and useful one….it will contain the nucleus of Denver's night life—restaurants, coffee houses, bars, nightclubs, off broadway (sic) theatre and jazz."

The letter went on to include specialty shops, art galleries, antique shops, artists' studios, elegant offices and residential space "…at fashionable rents for students working in the area and for those of cultural bent…all working together to give Denver the reputation for being a light hearted city."

Gibson liked the concept and pulled out his extensive Rolodex. He brought in Jim and Patricia Schroeder, two recent Harvard Law School graduates who had just moved to Denver. Pat, exceptionally smart and with a contagious laugh, would spend 24 years in Congress representing Denver and was one of the first women to seriously consider running for president.

"We didn't have any qualms about investing with her, it was something that needed to be done," Pat recalled recently from her home in Florida. "The New Yorker had run a sad article, to us, about Denver and how it didn't honor its past because it was tearing down all those old buildings. Dana was trying to save that part of downtown by taking on City Hall. And we loved the people she had assembled."

The Schroeders contributed $25,000, which Pat called "not a great investment" considering how long it took them to be repaid, which they were, in full.

Attorney Pat Schroeder, one of the original investors in Larimer Square, talks with an unidentified man on Larimer Street in the 1960s. Schroeder was the first woman from Colorado elected to Congress, representing Colorado's 1st District which includes Denver, and served 24 years until retiring in 1997. Diana DeGette won the vacant seat and still serves. Known for her sense of humor, Schroeder titled her memoir "24 Years of House Work… and the Place is Still a Mess: My Life in Politics."

Courtesy, ©James O. Milmoe

Gibson also brought in retired Col. Ralph Saltsman, Douglas Carruthers, Jack and Mary Temple, David Dunklee, Catherine Sue Morrison, architect Langdon Morris, realtor Harris Kelly and a Mr. X, whose name Dana says she can't remember. All of them signed up at the start. Ten years later, Carruthers, the Temples, Morris and Mr. X had withdrawn from the project. So had John Wootten, Rike's brother.

Eventually, Gibson's higher-ups at Boettcher heard about his dealings with Dana and Larimer Street and asked him to stop, Dana recalled. "They too thought it was a stupid idea and they didn't want any of their people involved in it." Gibson never invested in the project.

In all, the corporation sold the 12 investors a total of 25,000 shares, at a face value of roughly $25 each, for a rough total of $625,000. Dana and John Crawford owned 2,725 shares with a rough value of $68,125.

The firm of Dana Crawford Inc. was incorporated on Aug. 28, 1964, with the name changed three months later to Larimer Square Inc.

Even with the influence of Wootten as an assistant VP at Colorado National Bank, the commercial loan officers at CNB wouldn't touch the project. So the directors approached the Central Bank and Trust, which had a beautiful Jacques Benedict-designed headquarters building half a block away on the southwest corner of 15th and Lawrence streets. Central Bank owned several of the lots in Larimer Square and, perhaps seeing some hope for its vacant properties, agreed to loan the corporation money. But even though Central Bank liked the project, it still would not take a risk on Dana, and made the loans contingent on Wootten, Congdon and other key investors personally guaranteeing the loans. Once the project became successful, Central Bank and Trust was quick to take some of the credit for "financing" Larimer Square, although it had taken no risks at all.

Everyone involved knew clearly that the entire project had been funded privately by Wootten, Congdon and others with their personal guarantees. In that sense, Larimer Square was started entirely with private investments, another distinction for Dana's pioneering efforts. The average purchase price for the real estate had been $16,000 per lot, with the buildings having very little value.

Dana making plans for Larimer Square, 1963.

By March 1965, the corporation had received promises from all but two of the owners of the 18 buildings to either sell or lease their properties to Larimer Square. The details still needed to be worked out and the contracts still needed to be signed but progress was being made. The two that wouldn't join the project were Sperte's Lafitte Restaurant on the northeast corner of 14th and Larimer, and the building south of The Market, at 1443 Larimer, which housed Crest Distributing, an office supply company owned by Joe Replin.

Replin was an enigma. A tiny, stooped figure not much taller than five feet, Replin had assembled a fortune over the years by buying empty buildings throughout downtown Denver, including two in the 1700 block of Curtis Street. He kept them empty, somehow not needing the income they could produce, and used them primarily to store junk he collected. His Crest Distributing Co., at 1443 Larimer, was primarily an office-supply store, but also an outlet for Replin to sell anything he wanted, from old composition notebooks to typewriter ribbons to sights for M79 grenade launchers.

Replin quoted Dana such a ridiculously high purchase price for 1443 Larimer that it made her gasp. She didn't have that kind of money and Replin knew it. Partly as a peace offering, and partly as an attempt to minimize the building's shabby appearance, Dana offered to paint the weathered façade for $100. Replin refused, saying he could get it done cheaper. Dana and her team would just have to work around Replin.

Meanwhile, Dick Gibson secreted Dana in the basement of Sperte's Lafitte Restaurant, where he introduced her to owner Joe Sperte, who had renovated the restaurant several years earlier and was doing quite well. "We told him our plan in the strictest confidentiality," she said.

Sperte saw the advantage of Dana's project for his popular restaurant. He refused to sell because he was making good money but agreed to join forces with her, and keep it a secret.

Just two days after Gibson and Dana walked out of Lafitte's, feeling good about their progress, Dana got a call from a Mort Margolin, a reporter at the Rocky Mountain News, who said Sperte had called his friend, Rocky columnist Pocky Marranzino, and told him about Dana's plans to assemble the buildings in the 1400 block of Larimer. It was Friday afternoon and Pocky's column was scheduled to run in Sunday's edition.

Dana panicked because not all of the contracts on the 16 other buildings had been signed yet. Nothing was firm.

"We were still in negotiations and it would be disastrous if it got out into the newspaper," Dana said. "I was hung over when I went down to the Rocky Saturday morning and met with the editor, Jack Foster, to plead with him to kill the story. If the remaining property owners found out what we were doing, they would raise their prices unreasonably high and kill the project.

"We called Pocky into the meeting. Foster said he understood the problem because the Rocky was acquiring property along Colfax in order to expand. But he also said that the newspaper business was to print the news."

The solution the three worked out was to run the story but not identify the 1400 block specifically. "It was a rather casual mention of some properties on Larimer Street that were being looked at for acquisition, possibly as part of plans for urban renewal," Dana said.

By May 1965, Dana was convinced she had sufficient control of the block that she could start renovating the buildings and looking for tenants. For help with the renovations, she hired architect Langdon Morris, one of the few architects in the city with experience in historic preservation. He had led the design team to separate the D&F Tower from the department store when Bill Zeckendorf wanted to move Daniels and Fisher to his retail development in Court House Square. Morris liked Dana's project so well that he became a minor investor in it.

She also hired photographer James Milmoe, a nationally acclaimed architectural photographer, to photographically record the exteriors of all the buildings, as they were, untouched, fronts and backs as well as the alleyways and walkways.

Photos: © James O. Milmoe

Another problem facing Dana was that the Denver Urban Renewal Authority, in January 1964, had designated 22 blocks for demolition, with the western boundary drawn right down the middle of the 1400 block of Larimer Street. In order to keep the bulldozers out, Dana had to convince DURA that Mayor Tom Currigan supported her project, she had to get the newspapers behind her and she had to show some income from the properties. She needed to officially launch her project as quickly as possible. (DURA would watch Larimer Square closely for two years, eventually decided it might become successful and reclassified the street as a "rehabilitation area.")

She also hired photographer James Milmoe, a nationally acclaimed architectural photographer, to photographically record the exteriors of all the buildings, as they were, untouched, fronts and backs as well as the alleyways and walkways.

Drawing on her success in public relations, perhaps with some of Zeckendorf's flair, she wanted to create a splash for her project. She had developed a strong working relationship with Mayor Tom Currigan, strong enough that she boldly asked the mayor if he would host her press conference in his office at City Hall. She then wrote invitations to civic leaders that appeared as if the Mayor had sent them out. She wrote to her investors that Mayor Currigan also sent invitations to all local media outlets, as well as national publications such as Time, Newsweek, Life, Business Week and The Wall Street Journal. These invitations masterfully created the impression that the City of Denver fully supported Larimer Square.

Currigan drew the line and told Dana that the press conference would not be held in City Hall, that it was a corporate project and its announcement should be held in the corporation's offices. But the corporation had no offices because everything had been done in Dana's house. She quickly got a couple of workers, went into the Granite Building on the corner of 15th and Larimer streets and "scrubbed up" one of the empty offices to look like corporate headquarters.

**Denver Post:
an attractive housewife...**

**Denver Post:
a slender brunette who
resembles Jackie Kennedy.**

On Saturday, May 22, 1965, the media crammed into the office for the press conference, and covered the event thoroughly the next day, with The Denver Post's headline blaring "City Officials Hail $1 Million Larimer Square." The Post brazenly called Dana "an attractive housewife," then followed a week later with a feature story describing her as "a 33-year-old slender brunette who resembles Jackie Kennedy." The story noted that Mrs. Kennedy was renovating the White House while Dana was renovating Larimer Square.

Dana Crawford discusses her early plans for Larimer Square with Mayor Tom Currigan, left, and investor Rike Wootten, in 1965.

Dana, ever the clever PR writer, wrote several op-ed pieces for local newspapers, including one for the Silver State Record, a monthly publication that described itself as "Colorado's First Historical Newspaper."

Dana wrote, "Instead of wrecking crews so often seen in old parts of cities today, rebuilding crews are seen; instead of the dirt and rubble of destruction, new bricks, paint and sandblasting are being used to revive the true colors of these 1859-1892 era buildings."

Total restoration of the block was never a consideration because of the cost. Instead, each building was renovated modestly and according to need, ranging from painting the exterior to digging a new foundation. Dana's husband, John, had been helping Dana where he could while working his geology job. But that would change as John got drawn deeper into his wife's project. "Professionally, John gave a lot of time to Larimer Square," she said. "If he were here today, he might say he 'sacrificed' to help the project, but he liked it."

John moved his geology office from 17th and Champa streets into Larimer Square and tried to work both his geology practice as well as getting Larimer Square off the ground. Gradually, he worked less and less on geology and more and more on the square.

Dana had started keeping the financial books, in pencil, until she was snowed under by the contractors, permits, licenses and finding tenants. So John worked with attorney Hardin Holmes and the accounting firm Arthur Young & Co. to set the books up properly. John kept them himself for quite a long time, and assumed responsibility for refinancing the project.

He also began working with architect Morris, who designed several brick arches to link various buildings together, as well as to create a rear courtyard on the east side of the block near 14th Street. Dana didn't care for the arches, which led to a squabble and finally the firing of Morris. They weren't accurate historically, but the American Institute of Architects, at its regional meeting in Salt Lake City honored Morris for his work in Larimer Square, creating "not a museum, but a viable urban space. Morris was the first of five architects she would use.

"Being so detail oriented like I am, hung up wanting everything to be right from my perspective, I'm sure it was difficult for everybody," she said. "John and I took some (disagreements) home, which wasn't a good idea. We wouldn't fight but we'd disagree on priorities and what should be done next. In the Sussex Building, we had to replace the elevator and we didn't agree on the timing of that. It's challenging when a couple (lives and) works together. But we didn't make big issues out of it. We'd get it worked out. We could talk well."

The corporation was strapped financially, at one point having less than $5,000 in the bank. Yet it continued to sign leases and to contract with workers for the renovations, even installing central heating and air conditioning systems. The influential members of the board of trustees worked diligently with Central Bank and Trust, which agreed to loan the corporation an additional $327,000, provided that board members Wootten and Congdon signed personal guarantees that the money would be repaid.

In the first two years of operation, the corporation ran up enormous debt, nearly $500,000. The directors re-organized it as a limited partnership, with Wootten and Congdon carrying most of the risk. Eventually, Dana and John were forced to take out a second mortgage on their home on Humboldt Street.

On an earlier visit to Gaslight Square in St. Louis, John and Dana left some marketing brochures about the upcoming Larimer Square, which caught the eye of Joel Schiavone, owner of a chain of six banjo/beer halls called "Your Father's Mustache." Schiavone flew to Denver and struck a deal with the Crawfords to open his seventh establishment in Larimer Square. The three became such good friends that Schiavone would stay with the Crawfords.

Liquor licenses had become difficult to acquire following Mayor Quigg Newton's crackdown aimed at stopping bribes being paid to city council members for new licenses. The city virtually stopped issuing new licenses, and adopted a policy that licenses could be transferred to a new location only if a need for a new bar could be justified. However, a number of Skid Row bars had been shut down in the area, so Schiavone was able to convince the city to give him a new license after a three-month wait.

"It's challenging when a couple (lives and) works together. But we didn't make big issues out of it. We'd get it worked out. We could talk well."

On Dec. 28, 1965, Your Father's Mustache opened its doors in the Frontenac Building at 1433 Larimer Street. Skeptics had said that nobody would come. Dana and John merely smiled as the line waiting to get in grew around the corner onto 15th Street. The real proof of their success came when Schiavone told the Crawfords the bar had grossed $4,000 in its first week, a record for his entire chain.

The real proof of their success came when Schiavone told the Crawfords the bar had grossed $4,000 in its first week, a record for his entire chain.

Courtesy, Crawford Collection

Courtesy, Crawford Collection

·LARIMER SQUARE MATURES·

"The most wonderful people

in the world are difficult,"

~ said Dana, on being dubbed "The Dragon Lady."

"I was so tired of people telling me Larimer Square would never work," Dana said. "Sandy Johnson of the University of Denver's business school said no one was going to come. No one would go to Skid Row."

When Your Father's Mustache opened on a cold, blustery night in late December 1965, the banjo/beer hall at 1433 Larimer Street filled up quickly. Soon a line of people waiting to get in formed down Larimer to 15th, went around the corner to Market Street and then halfway down Market. "It was a huge success," Dana said. "The banjo music was perfect."

By the end of the week, the Mustache's owner Joel Schiavone told the Crawfords that the Denver bar had grossed more than $4,000 in the first week, more than his six other Mustache bars had ever individually grossed.

The Crawfords were pleased, even giddy, about their initial success. But the crush of work to be done weighed heavily and prevented them from taking a deep breath.

The next 20 years would take them on a rich and rewarding ride, yet they also would be dragged into hassles, double-crossings, anger, disagreements, confrontations with lawyers, and the courts. Their successes would be hard-fought and not easily won.

Dana and John worked themselves to exhaustion making Larimer Square a success. At times, events overwhelmed the pair, negating Dana's obsession to control everything. Occasionally there were disastrous consequences, totally beyond their control.

But for the most part, running Larimer Square over two decades was a glorious experience that would bring national exposure and praise to the Crawfords and Colorado.

Schiavone welcomed his first crowd in Larimer Square by telling them that Denver is "a city with a reputation for being young at heart." Dana took the stage and told the crowd to expect more high-quality entertainment like this, that Larimer Square would never have go-go clubs, strip joints or 3.2 beer places, which attracted teenagers. The Denver Post called Your Father's Mustache a "loud, happy, brassy sing-along pub."

In January, a month after the pub opened, four more shops signed leases and began to move in: Gusterman's Silversmiths (which is still open); the Blue Bottle Tree, which sold three-dimensional stained and leaded glass objects; Poor Richard's leather goods; and the Gondola Boutique, for ski and sportswear. All of them opened in the Bull and Bear courtyard in the southeast portion of the block, named for the two sandstone sculptures that had been moved to the courtyard from the Mining Exchange Building at 15th and Arapahoe streets before it was torn down. The images characterized investors' attitudes on Wall Street.

Bull and Bear terra cotta sculptures taken from the Mining Exchange building as it was being torn down in the early 1960s. The stock-market icons now watch over the Bull and Bear courtyard behind the Kettle Building, at the entrance to the Bistro Vendome restaurant.

Photo: Melanie Simonet

Gusterman's, now the Square's longest tenant, was started in Georgetown by Swedes Astrid and Stig Gusterman. Mary Eckels started working in the shop in 1976, then bought it two years later. Only in her 20s when she took over, Eckels had never owned a business before. She feared she was in over her head when Dana presented her with a 35-page lease for a 900-square-foot store.

"I was afraid of Dana. She was so powerful, but friendly," Eckels said. "I called the office to explain to me a few things about the lease. Dana came over and spent the afternoon explaining everything to me. It was a lovely thing to do."

—————

"We worked very hard," Dana said. "We started renting out the first floors of the buildings in January. We had opening after opening after opening. We had a fundraiser for local charities every time something opened. Finally, John said, 'I'll never go to another opening.'"

"The newspapers made Larimer Square," she added. "They loved it." The Denver Post's business editor, Willard Hazelbush, dubbed it "Denver's new fun street." Dana rolls her eyes skyward talking about Hazelbush, whom she adored but described as "a huge drinker who took notes on matchbook covers." Hazelbush would order endless Bloody Marys while interviewing Dana. More than once, she asked the bartender to serve her only one Bloody Mary with booze and make the rest of them Virgin Marys.

—————

Dana and John originally planned to renovate only the east side of Larimer Street for the first few years. But that changed when Schiavone, without explaining himself, said he liked the space in 1433 Larimer on the west side of the street. The Crawfords leased it to him. He bought the liquor license of a nearby café that was closing and opened his speakeasy.

None of the buildings in the 1400 block were original because of a massive fire in 1863 that leveled every building made of wood. But the block had been rebuilt before 1900, with many buildings showing cornerstones dating between 1871 and 1873.

Dana and John were surprised to learn, after they purchased the Kettle Building at 1426 Larimer, that it had no side walls. Apparently, George Kettle bought an 18-foot-wide piece of land in 1873, then cheaply built front and back walls, as well as a roof, which he attached to the neighboring buildings on each side.

Dana's favorite building on the block initially was the Sussex Hotel, at 1430-34 Larimer, where she fancied putting upscale apartments on the upper floors. It held Denver's first post office, and the first barbershop, where Horace Greeley allegedly stopped in for a shave and trim.

Dana and John constantly tried to find the right balance between small, interesting and unique shops run by artisans and crafts people, and the much larger, noisy and higher-grossing restaurants and bars. Within the first few months of its opening, Larimer Square proved to be a popular place for daytime shopping and nighttime dining and drinking. The Crawfords' risky venture was beginning to pay off as more and more business owners wanted to lease space there. In the early years of Larimer Square, the Crawfords leased everything through their own corporate office and never paid a broker's fee.

Richard Pinhorn honored by Larimer Street Business Improvement. Dana Crawford and Rabbi Earl Stone.

In the spring of 1966, Denver attorney Larry Atler and others brought to Larimer Square a successful restaurant concept from Chicago and opened the Bratskellar, a German beer stube with two large fireplaces, one outside on a subterranean patio. Later, his team would open Josephina's across the street where Your Father's Mustache had been. Atler and his team eventually opened restaurants in eight American cities and were highly successful.

One of the more elegant restaurants to open was the 1421 Club, with three themes: The Palm Court, for drinking and light dining in an airy room with a stained-glass skylight and potted trees and vines; L'Orangerie, the main dining room; and The Library, a private room decorated with cherrywood paneling that one of the owners, Shelley Don, salvaged from the Bonfils Mansion on the west edge of Cheesman Park. Ironically, The Library was used mostly as a discotheque. Many considered it the premier nightspot in Larimer Square, crowded with attractive women and well-dressed men, until it closed 18 months after it opened.

Most of the Square's restaurants and bars were noisy and fun places. A more elegant restaurant that appealed to an older crowd was Café Promenade, located on the lower level of the Bull and Bear courtyard.

The patio of Café Promenade in the Bull and Bear courtyard in the rear of the Kettle Building, 1428 Larimer St.

Courtesy, Crawford Collection

Courtesy, Tish Kllanxhja

(left)
Tish Kllanxhja
owner of Café
Promenade and
(right) Fred Thomas
maître d', of Café
Promenade.

Tish Kllanxhja (kah lan' ja) was an Albanian-born opera singer in New York City whose singing career was short-lived. Enchanted with singing restaurants and unable to get a start in New York, he and his friend, Mario Lalli, on a tip drove four days out to Aspen, which was just beginning to boom with skiers in 1952. They bought a vacant restaurant and set up an Italian menu served by singing waiters. Tish followed his unhappy wife back to New York in 1956 but it wasn't enough to save their marriage. Mario, who had been the more hesitant of the two to drive to Aspen, turned his namesake restaurant, Mario's, into an Aspen standard for the next 40 years.

Tish returned to Denver and worked at the Columbine Country Club a short while before taking over the University Club in 1960. He was a natural manager and people pleaser. In 1965, John Crawford, a member of the University Club, approached him about opening a restaurant in the soon-to-open Larimer Square. Dana found some investors, notably Tom Congdon, Bill Miller, Fred Hamilton and other oil men, and developed Café Promenade into a high-end, very popular restaurant. It had an outdoor patio for the warmer months.

The café had no bar, just tables and chairs, and served French/Italian/European food. Tish later claimed to have the largest wine cellar in the city. For 15 years, Tish managed both the University Club restaurant and Café Promenade, working sometimes 20 hours a day, walking between the two venues several times a day.

For the front man, or maître d', Tish hired Fred Thomas, an imposing figure at 6'5" and 350 pounds who loved practical jokes. With a booming, baritone voice, he'd greet his favorites, "Good Evening, Mr. and Mrs. XXXXX, and how many will there be in your party of two?" He once announced to the entire restaurant that the White House was on the phone, wondering why so-and-so (some high-profile customer eating in the restaurant) wouldn't return its calls. "Shall I put them through now?" he'd ask to loud laughter

One snowy evening, with customers waiting in the cold to get in, Fred Thomas opened the door and was told, "Fred, there's a U.S. Senator (Gordon Allott) waiting to get in." Thomas shot back, "We've already got one (Peter Dominick) inside," and closed the door.

As the ground-floor spaces of Larimer Square were renovated and leased out, John and Dana began refurbishing offices on the second and third floors. Dana had wanted apartments but settled on elegant offices, which attracted an interesting mix of tenants, including a number of lawyers. One was Bruce Ducker, a lawyer and novelist who was building a new law firm after having been president of Great Western United Corporation until the Hunt brothers from Texas took it over.

"We had two lawyers, a couple of $30 cases and some small stuff," he joked. The firm would grow to 30 lawyers and Ducker would write his first novel there: *Rule by Proxy*, which attracted two national publishing houses before he sold it to Crown.

"Sometimes when I worked late, Fred would see my lights on and send a waiter up the stairs with a tray of oxtail soup, bread and a split of wine. It was wonderful," he said.

Another tenant was David French, a developer who played critical roles in saving the D&F Tower and locating the Convention Center downtown. He and his team rented four offices across the hall from Lonnie Grant's modeling agency. "These very pretty girls would come in looking for Lonnie," French said. "We'd tell them she's busy, have a seat. They were very pretty, young girls, all dressed up. You'd hope they'd make it."

Jock Bickert rented space next to Ducker. He owned National Demographics & Lifestyles, which he claimed was the first company to compile demographic data on millions of consumers, then sort out their buying patterns for clients like Nikon, Sony, Panasonic and others.

"Larimer Square back then was magical," Bickert said. "I likened it to my idea of what Paris must be like…shopkeepers opening their stores and sweeping the sidewalks, tenants arriving for work fresh from a good night's sleep. Everyone was bustling with energy, ready to start the day. You knew them all, you'd stop to chat a while, it was high energy. And when I finally traveled to Paris, it was exactly as I had imagined."

The Square became a popular place for renting small offices, including a few high-profile tenants. Gary Hart officed there before unseating incumbent U.S. Senator Peter Dominick in 1974. Another was lawyer/lobbyist Craig Barnes, best known for running Colorado Common Cause.

Café Promenade was a favorite of Denver's upper crust and made a lot of money off of oil men and others on large expense accounts. But when the oil market crashed in the mid-1980s, the restaurant's business slowed considerably. That caused problems for everyone, especially Tish and Fred, who felt the Café had become too high-end.

"I sold it to Dana (and partner Charles Callaway) in 1987," Tish said. "I didn't get any equity. By the time I had paid everybody what was owed, I was left with three or four thousand dollars."

Tom Congdon, who had invested $15,000 in Café Promenade, laughed. "It became successful and we all got paid back. The only profit we received on our investment was one free dinner every year. Tish and Fred got brand new cars every year, eventually moving up to Mercedes. Hell, we didn't care. We just wanted a good table. Being an owner gave us the clout to get a good table."

Ducker told a similar story: "When they shut down Café Promenade, they gave away a bunch of liquor. I overheard one guy with a case of wine say, 'This is the first dividend I've received.'"

Concerned about the overall image and success of Larimer Square, John and Dana were picky about the tenants they would accept. Their stores had to be outfitted tastefully and needed a high-quality product line. And they had to be profitable. No detail was too small for Dana. She demanded final approval over the stores' motif, wall colors, signs, printed materials and advertisements.

Rents were based on a percentage of gross sales, with a minimum base rent due each month. The rents were determined by the businesses' quarterly tax returns. If the numbers were in doubt, Dana demanded an audit of the store's books.

She was quoted in one of the newspapers: "In an area like this you have to set standards of quality and maintain control. We want Larimer Square here 100 years from now, and control is the only way a project like this can succeed."

Kurt Wendt owned a high-quality wool and linen fabrics store in the Square in 1969. But his business was slow, grossing only about $11,000 a year, and Dana evicted him for not meeting a minimum annual sales amount.

"I must say I was extremely excited about what I saw in Larimer Square in the early days," Wendt told the Rocky Mountain News. "But arts and crafts mean slow money. A high quality artist takes his time to work. I am a high caliber weaver. I start with a thread.

"If they (the Crawfords) would take their time and wait for the money to come in, I would still be there. I feel she didn't have the ability to see the difference between the output of a craftsman and the souvenirs in a souvenir store."

Smartly, he found a new location for much less rent only a block away, at 1437 Market Street, which was close enough to take advantage of the overflow of the crowds Larimer Square was attracting.

Joel Kunkel, general manager of the Royal Platte River Yacht Club, a somewhat rowdy restaurant and dance hall on the northwest corner of 14th and Larimer, was quite frank in an interview with the Rocky Mountain News. He said his lawyer was astounded at the complexity and thoroughness of Kunkel's 30-page lease, calling it tough, all-encompassing and "very, very legal."

The lease required Kunkel to pay 6 percent gross of all food sales and 8 percent gross of all liquor sales, plus water, electricity, insurance and other expenses. Dana gave him three years to reach gross annual sales of $400,000 or he would be evicted, according to the article. Dana had her designers pick the interior colors of the restaurant, and kept approval rights over his menu, graphics, printed materials and advertisements.

"There's just no tolerance in the lease for a business that isn't running at maximum capacity," Kunkel told the News.

Fred Thomas at Café Promenade was equally frank with the reporter but more at ease because of the Café's success. "She is a very good businesswoman, and you have to be a callous witch to be a very good businesswoman. I have great admiration and respect for her," he said. "Businesswise, she's done a very good job in the Square. The reason it's here is because she's….single-minded." Café Promenade, by comparison, grossed more than $700,000 in 1974 and paid roughly $50,000 in annual rent.

The Rocky Mountain News, in a different article on June 20, 1974, said merchants in the Square had started referring to Dana as "The Dragon Lady" for her tactics in controlling the tenants. The line came from a newspaper cartoon "Terry and the Pirates" by Milton Caniff.

How ironic it was for this small-town Kansas girl, who grew up wearing white gloves and Easter bonnets wanting to please everyone, who was selected into five national honor societies and who was the happily married mother of four young boys, now to be weighted with such a dark reputation. She persevered but the moniker would stick on her for decades.

"They say I'm tough. Well, I hate that word 'tough', especially when used on a woman. It makes me think of Burt Lancaster," she told the newspaper.

Photo by Sarah Cook. Courtesy, Crawford Collection

Dana is now dubbed "The Dragon Lady."

More recently, she looked back on the difficult times with a clearer perspective. "We struggled every day with money issues. We had to pay our loans," she said.

Some tenants defended her. David French, who opened a short-lived wine store in the back of the Granite Building, said, "Dana used to encourage us to keep trying. She did that with a lot of people with a lot of disparate businesses. A lot of them didn't work."

"If she could have collected all the rent she was owed, she'd be living in Paris," he added.

Even Tish Kllanxhja fell behind in his rent at the beloved Café Promenade when the "oil business went to hell." He tried to sell the restaurant, but Dana encouraged him to keep trying and, as an investor in the restaurant, turned down several buyers. "Even when I couldn't meet my obligations to Dana, I never had a problem with her," he said. Eventually, he sold out to the Crawfords in 1987.

Fabby Hillyard became another powerful female in downtown Denver and remained somewhat in awe of Dana. Hillyard wasn't a private developer like Dana, but rose in the city's administration, from being an early fundraiser for Wellington Webb's mayoral campaigns to Manager of Theaters and Arenas, where she oversaw the expansion of the convention center, the creation of the visitors' center at Red Rocks and the conversion of the Auditorium into the Ellie Caulkins Opera House. She had projects underway at one time estimated at $500 million.

"Dana is very intense, she can terrify people," Hillyard said. "She can be really mean. She doesn't tolerate stupidity, and she's the judge of what's stupid. She's very competitive and such a strong force that people don't call her on it.

"But Dana works harder than anyone I have ever known. She's so smart and fearless when she has a good idea. She will make it happen. All of these are hugely admirable qualities in business. But they don't make you a great number of friends."

Larimer Square caught on quickly, both locally and nationally, and became a popular stop for visitors and tourists. The locals, particularly the singles crowd, devoured it because the bars were noisy and packed, with plenty of music and fun. It became the hot spot for picking up the opposite sex, and quite a few marriages were spawned at night in early Larimer Square. A few of them still are together.

Comedian Pat Paulsen came through Larimer Square in August 1968, during his run for the presidency. Some 2,500 people came to hear Paulsen, who called his campaign the Straight Talking American Government (STAG) Party. "We should take crime out of the streets and put it back in the homes, where it started," he told the crowd. When he was criticized for being able to throw a half-dollar only halfway across the Potomac River, he fired back, "Money doesn't go as far today."

Lady Bird Johnson, the nation's First Lady, visited Larimer Square on a "farewell" tour of the country in 1968 after her husband, President Lyndon Johnson, announced he would not seek re-election. Lady Bird had pushed a program of "beautification," which included cleaning roadways, planting wildflowers and generally preserving the nation's natural and historic resources. As Dana escorted her through some of Larimer Square's shops, the First Lady publicly thanked Dana and John for their work in revitalizing a run-down part of the city.

Lady Bird Johnson, 2nd from left, visits Larimer Square in 1968, just months before she and her husband, President Lyndon Johnson, left the White House. Dana, right, explains her preservation efforts.

When Larimer Square faced adversity, Dana drew on her formidable marketing skills to turn a challenge into an advantage. About five years after the Square opened, the City of Denver had to replace the sewer line. The excavators dug a large trench right down the center of Larimer Street, and piled the dirt 16' high down the sides of the trench. "I was just sitting there, staring at this pile of dirt and we had no customers," she said. "It pretty much shut us down. One day it snowed, so I got the idea and had a poster made that said 'Ski Larimer Square.'"

Among the myriad of details that came up in the operation of such a large project was Dana's salary. John Crawford had been doing the bookkeeping for the square, without a calculator, and, mistakenly or not, wrote that Dana was being paid $1.25 per hour. Rike Wootten and other board members objected and said she should be making much more than that. However, upon further inspection, the books showed that Dana was taking home $10,000 annually. Someone pointed out that she couldn't be making $1.25 an hour because she would have to work 22 hours a day to make $10,000 a year. At times, she felt she was.

As news of Larimer Square's success spread, officials from other cities began flying to Denver, almost weekly, to ask Dana how they might start something similar in their towns. Suddenly, she was much in demand and ended up consulting for some 50 cities across the country. She became involved in the development of Underground Atlanta, Boston's Quincy Marketplace, New York's South Street Seaport complex, and cities such as Savannah, San Antonio and Charleston, S.C.

Growth and financial stability did not come easily for Larimer Square. It started out as a $1 million project, with roughly 200,000 square feet of rentable space. Half of that was used to create some 70 offices and the other half was for retail sales, including 9 restaurants and 35 shops. Initially, the corporation was able to borrow roughly $500,000 for construction costs from Central Bank and Trust Co., which required personal signatures, double collateral of oil and gas properties offered as security, and a second mortgage on the Crawford home.

Both John and Dana put significant effort into finding long-term financing for the Square. After numerous refusals, they were able to borrow nearly $2 million from the New York Life Insurance Co. in 1972. It was reported to be the first loan ever made to a historic district under one ownership and with a proven operating history.

"It was the first time in the U.S. for this. It was a very big achievement," said Dana, who explained that it had been treated in part as a "minority" loan because of her involvement. "And we were told later that we were the only ones ever to repay" a minority loan of this kind.

The New York Life money took some of the pressure off the Crawfords and their limited-partner investors. But the loan came with restrictions about the operation of the Square, including specific goals for renovating and leasing the remaining empty properties. If the leasing was going too slowly, or not at all, the lender could cancel the entire loan. That was cause for concern and put a premium on finding proper tenants who would fit the Square's image and generate enough gross sales to pay the required rent.

More than once, the leasing deadline would be upon them, with no new tenants that Dana liked. So she solved that dilemma, fearlessly, by starting her own businesses, becoming both a tenant and the landlord. She would do this six times and in 1982 was producing 10 percent of the square's rental income.

"The most successful business I started was Victoriana Antique and Fine Jewelry," she said. "Every month, I went to Washington, D.C. for board meetings with the National Trust (for Historic Preservation). I stayed in the Hay-Adams Hotel across from the White House. A store there called 'The Little Jewel Box' had the greatest stuff. I met the owner and paid him his hourly appraisal rate to answer pages and pages of my questions about his business. In the end, he told me, 'If you find something really precious, it doesn't matter how much it costs. Find the money and buy it.'

"I needed a partner to help run it for me so I found Audrey Stehlin, who was very knowledgeable. We would find jewelry in pawn shops which we bought and resold. Eventually people would come in with their jewelry for us to sell on consignment. Our store was 300 square feet and produced the highest sales per-square-foot in the Square."

She kept the store for nearly four years before selling it to David and Veronica Prebble, who still operate it in Larimer Square.

Another, much larger business that Dana started was The Market, which would cause her endless headaches, including the eviction of a restaurant owner and a substantial financial loss.

"The original idea was from Pike Place Market in Seattle, where there were lots of small operators selling their goods," she said. The first mistake she made was to hire an architectural student at the University of Colorado-Denver to design the market. It never created enough energy to attract customers and soon failed. It became known as the "Flop Market."

The Market, started by Dana, at 1445 Larimer St.

THE MARKET

At the same time, Specialty Food Magazine came out with a picture of the first Dean & DeLuca grocery store in New York City, which opened in 1977 and had exactly the look and feel Dana wanted. Dana flew to New York, met with the three partners and then hosted Giorgio DeLuca in Denver. Surveying the site in the Square, the New Yorker's first remark was, "Where are all the people?" But he liked Dana's enthusiasm and the three other people she had hired to help her—Helen Finklestein, Rob Austin-Murphy and Tess O'Brien. DeLuca agreed to train the four of them in New York for three weeks.

Dana's son, Tom Crawford, was living in New York and found an apartment for the quartet on Prince Street in SoHo, close to the Dean & DeLuca store. The four visitors from Denver were excited about their SoHo adventure, but first they were to experience some of New York's harsher realities.

"The apartment had never been cleaned," Dana said. "There were mice and turds everywhere. Tom hadn't noticed. I said, 'I can't stay here. It will take two weeks just to clean.'"

That evening, they ran into Olivia Emery, a Denver woman who had grown up close to the Crawford house and knew Dana's sons. Emery, a Yale-educated architect working in New York, met Dana's team for dinner in a nice trattoria, where she recommended they buy a case of grapefruit and cut it into pieces. "At least the apartment will smell better," she said.

"I spent one night there, with the cockroaches. I slept in my raincoat," Dana said. The next day, she and Helen "found an old hotel up by the Museum of Natural History." Rob and Tess stayed in the apartment, which had been paid for in advance.

"We spent three weeks in New York, but Dean & DeLuca didn't really have time to train us," Dana added. "I met a guy named George Kinsler, who had developed a fabulous kitchen store in the basement of Macy's. He showed us how to slice a ham, how to wrap it and other things. We drank every night and laughed a lot."

Austin-Murphy still has pleasant memories of the trip. "Dana had this idea that she could bring this concept (Dean & DeLuca) to Denver. We all had this sense of creating something wonderful," he said. "But she's a party girl, as well as a businesswoman. We went out and had beautiful food, nice glasses of wine; it was a mix of pleasure and work that was beautifully woven together."

Back in Denver, Dana struggled with the city's health inspectors. "They couldn't decide if The Market was a grocery store or a restaurant," she said. "They decided it was both and required us to have a 3-hole sink every 15 feet (in the food preparation area). When Mayor Bill McNichols came down for the dedication, he asked, 'Why all these sinks.' I told him the inspectors required them. He said I should have called the Manager of Heath."

Tess O'Brien had been managing the store but didn't like it. So Dana called her friend Tish at Café Promenade for help finding someone to run The Market. On his recommendation, Dana hired Jim Eskridge, the food and beverage manager at the University Club. He liked the concept of The Market, so he flew to New York to study the "rhythm" of Dean & DeLuca's.

The Chinese restaurant "Antonio Tsai" in the basement of The Market, 1445 Larimer Street.

Eskridge proved very adept at making changes that worked and the store began to improve. "But every time I asked the accountant if we were making a profit, she'd say, 'We had a positive cash flow,'" Eskridge recalled.

The basement of the market was a large, empty space that needed to be rented. Blair Chotzinoff, a New York boulevardier and former lover of Gloria Steinem, had moved to Denver and complained about missing his favorite Chinese restaurant. He heard about Larimer Square, about the available space and soon, New York restaurateur Antonio Tsai arrived in Denver, ready to make a culinary splash.

Rob Austin-Murphy designed an attractive restaurant for Tsai in the basement of The Market. The build-out cost four times more than the amount budgeted and the finished product, outfitted in gleaming white tile, looked nothing like a Chinese restaurant. But "Antonio Tsai" opened to great reviews in April 1981.

Despite his pedigree, having claimed to cook for the family of Chiang Kai-shek, Tsai had little tolerance for the mundane aspects of the business. One day, a black delivery truck driver carried in boxes of dishes and glassware and misunderstood where he thought Tsai, in broken English, had told him to put them. The driver went back outside for more when Tsai angrily grabbed some of the boxes and threw them into the alley, breaking everything, according to Eskridge, who was managing the restaurant. The driver told Tsai he would have to sign for the broken stuff and a fight broke out. Tsai grabbed a meat cleaver and threatened the driver.

Eskridge was able to stop the volatile Tsai, then called the supply house and worked things out. Dana the next day fired Eskridge for not being able to handle Tsai, according to Eskridge. Tsai was ordered out of the building, never to return.

Several months later, Tsai found a job cooking a block away on Market Street and his namesake restaurant in the basement of The Market soon closed.

The Market never worked out well for Dana. "It was designed for people—managers, employees and customers—to steal. I got rid of a lot of employees. I cleaned it on the weekends. I worked so hard. I had it one year and lost about $350,000."

The sidewalk clock tower in front of The Market. Dana and John Crawford purchased the clock, then moved it from the 1500 block of Larimer Street to save it from being demolished by DURA.

Photo: Melanie Simonet

The 14' tall Brown Street Clock was built in 1910 and originally installed in front of the Manhattan Restaurant at 1627 Larimer. It was destined to be destroyed in DURA's demolitions, so John, Dana and a friend with a truck removed the clock at just after midnight one morning—(it's unknown how much alcohol was involved)—and carried it up to 1445 Larimer, in front of The Market.

Railroad pensioners, with a penchant for drink, lived upstairs at 1445. Several days later, two pensioners sitting on the entrance stairs noticed the clock. "I don't remember that clock being there," said one. "Oh you fool," replied the other. "It's been there for years!"

"There were so many things just so hideously difficult," Dana said, recalling the fiasco with The Market. "I was juggling so many frickin balls. There were only so many fights I could fight."

Two brothers, Mark and Gary Greenberg, who owned a whole-sale cheese business, bought The Market from Dana in 1983 and made it work. Gary died in November 2000. But Mark can still be found there every day, running it smoothly.

———————————

With her talent for public relations, Dana continued to invent new promotions and clever campaigns for the Square. Learning of the large number of Coloradans with German heritage, and capitalizing on the Bratskellar's and other restaurants' popularity, she started Denver's Oktoberfest, held the last weekend in September and the first in October, as in Munich, to avoid the colder weather. Lufthansa Airlines contributed to the event, as did the Adolph Coors Co. The city allowed the street to be closed and issued a liquor license. Among the hundreds of people Dana would mentor in her life, she had a young man, John Gray, learning PR from her and acting as a gopher. So she instructed him to build a bandstand for Oktoberfest.

The first weekend was a huge success, with glorious weather and large crowds quaffing gallons of beer and dancing in the street. Many wore lederhosen and busty dirndl dresses.

The second week was a disaster. Saturday morning, the temperature plummeted so low that the musicians couldn't put the brass instruments to their lips. The band couldn't oompah but nobody wanted to drink and party outside anyway. To make matters worse, Dana and John Crawford had violated some section of the liquor code and were told they would not be allowed to sell the beer leftover from the first weekend. So they offered free suds to anyone who came down that chilly weekend. Word got around and enough freezing partiers eventually gathered to finish off the final keg.

As for her protégé, John Gray, his bandstand fell apart the first weekend. Dana jokingly told him to go back to school and learn something, which he did. Recently, he was named director of the Smithsonian Institution's National Museum of American History and he still keeps in touch with Dana.

Dana loved the marketing side of her work, and was very creative with it. She and John continued to come up with new events that would draw crowds, like bagpipers on St. Patrick's Day, Sunday art markets and the Colorado Springs Symphony Orchestra playing the 1812 Overture, with bells and cannons. She even convinced the radical, avant garde theatrical director, Peter Sellars, who was working at the Elitch Gardens theater one summer, to give performances of Wagner's Ring Cycle operas in the Square.

Dana also went to the expense and effort of purchasing two, bright-red, double-decker Bristol buses in Europe and shipping them from Antwerp to Newark, N.J., where The New York Times covered their arrival on July 17, 1969. She sent seven college students from Denver to drive them cross-country. Averaging 30 miles per hour, the trip took eight days. Dana and her family joined the buses in Chicago but Dana and John jumped off in St. Louis out of boredom.

The buses became popular sights in downtown Denver, offering free trips to Larimer Square. Dana successfully used them to ferry members of the National Trust for Historic Preservation when the group held its annual meeting in Denver. She also offered the buses to nonprofit groups for use at charity events.

Dana's highly visible London taxicab, in which she drove friends, investors and sightseers around Denver for many years.

In the same vein, Dana had always loved riding in black, boxy London cabs. When she learned about a mechanic in Detroit who was converting them with left-side steering wheels for use in America, Dana bought one immediately and drove it for years through the streets of downtown Denver.

As Larimer Square began attracting large crowds, the spillover began to draw the attention of other developers. One of them was George "Geoie" Writer, who in 1978 paid roughly $1 million for the entire block across 15th Street from Larimer Square, between Larimer and Lawrence streets. The Denver Urban Renewal Authority had paved it over for parking lots and was not maintaining it well.

Over the next three years, the Writer Corp. built Writer Square, which encompassed 47 retail spaces and 42 relatively expensive condominiums. Its total square footage was slightly smaller than Larimer Square, but Writer Square had residential units and underground parking. The layout had a large walkway leading from the Tabor Center at 16th and Lawrence streets diagonally through the square to the corner of Larimer Square at 15th and Larimer streets. It was a very smart development that greatly benefitted all three projects.

By the mid-1980s, Denver had added the 16th Street pedestrian mall with a free shuttle bus, the Tabor Center, Writer Square, Larimer Square and the redeveloped Tivoli Brewery building on the Auraria campus. Despite the shaky economy, Larimer Square had developed enough momentum that national retail chains began looking at branch stores there.

Dana had always wanted the retailer May D&F to open a store in the Granite Building on 15th Street, where the May Co. had its first store in Denver in the 1800s. That never happened but she did convince Williams-Sonoma to open a two-story kitchenware store in the Granite Building. Other national tenants that followed were Laura Ashley, Ylang Ylang jewelry, Ann Taylor, Marimekko fabrics and Talbots.

As Larimer Square became more and more profitable, Dana was able to loosen her white-knuckled grip on the Square and begin looking at other opportunities. One idea that interested her was residential housing near the Square. She told Joanne Ditmer of The Denver Post in September 1982 that she had always thought of Larimer Square "as a place in search of a neighborhood." Larimer Square Associates, Dana's group, owned four lots on the east side of the 1400 block of Market Street. In a letter to the partners on Oct. 11, 1982, she proposed buying four adjacent lots south to 14th Street, as well as the triangular piece of land that the old city hall had sat on south of 14th Street between Larimer and Market streets.

This project, if successful, would take Dana out of preservation and into the world of large-scale, commercial development of new buildings, contrary to how she had made her reputation.

On Market Street, she proposed building a 16-story, 400-unit residential building, an enormous parking garage and office and retail space nearly equal to one-quarter of all rental space in Larimer Square. For the triangular piece of property, she proposed building a 200-room bed-and-breakfast style hotel or inn. That development, to be called Larimer Square Equities, would then purchase all of Larimer Square for $20 million.

The Rocky Mountain News attacked the plan in an editorial on Dec. 5, 1982, primarily because it would include a $5 million grant from the Colorado Housing and Finance Authority. Mayor Bill McNichols didn't like it nor did Federico Peña, who was elected to succeed McNichols as mayor in 1983. Even some of Dana's partners in Larimer Square Associates objected to the plan. It never materialized, but did introduce the idea of selling Larimer Square.

In the meantime, in order to protect the future of Larimer Square, Dana had worked with Historic Denver, city staff and city council to introduce the concept of transferable development rights (TDRs) or "air rights" over historic buildings. They were introduced as a means of protecting smaller, historic buildings when the land they sit on becomes more valuable than the buildings. The owner of a historic building who has the right to add floors to the building could take those "air rights" and "transfer" or sell them to another building owner who might be restricted by zoning laws from topping off his building. The value of the air rights would be determined by the value the additional floors would add to the original building.

Through a long and involved process and with the help of architect Michael Barber, Dana had identified and registered the substantial TDRs for Larimer Square, which had grown quite valuable in 1983. A developer interested in demolishing three buildings at 17th and Champa streets negotiated to buy some of the Square's TDRs. But as he hesitated, the real estate market dropped precipitously and the air rights lost much of their value.

Dana turned to selling Larimer Square as a viable commercial enterprise. The Post's Joanne Ditmer reported that rents had risen from 11 cents a square foot in 1965 to $15-$20 per square foot in 1985. In 1986, the Trizec Hahn Corp., a large shopping-center operator based in San Diego, which had recently purchased the Tivoli Center across Speer Boulevard, bought Larimer Square for $14.5 million. The deal included a small percentage of the available TDRs.

In short, the Square sold as a viable commercial enterprise operating in a designated historic district that had gone through extensive preservation efforts and succeeded. It proved the adage that historic buildings could be repurposed and become profitable.

===========

Bill Mosher, who headed the Downtown Denver Partnership for about 10 years, witnessed Dana's impact on the transformation of lower downtown.

"I've always viewed Dana as a person who understands cities and understands the dynamic, messy nature of cities," Mosher said. "Dana knew people had to express their opinions and that people bring different things to the table, whether they're young or old, new to the area, architects or historic preservationists. Dana always understood the nature of the fray."

===========

"John and my family were patient with me. I wasn't always where they wanted me to be as a wife and a mother," said Dana, on balancing work and family.

Larimer Square took off faster in its first two years than anyone had imagined, including the Crawfords. Store owners wanted every available space. Renovation crews couldn't work fast enough and John Crawford scrambled among investors, bankers and pension funds looking for more money to maintain the growth.

By 1967, the Crawford family was growing just as fast, with four rambunctious boys, ages 7, 9, 10 and 11, growing evermore curious about their surroundings and developing the courage to start exploring. The boys were getting bigger, stronger and wilder; boundaries for each of them were becoming a necessity. Their four-bedroom house at 629 Humboldt was beginning to look like a refugee camp.

"After 11 years in 629 Humboldt, we were bursting at the seams," Dana said. "So in 1967 we began to look for a bigger house. Katie Billings, a dear friend and a real estate broker, showed me 685 Emerson, a huge, three-story house for sale for $41,000. It had been turned into a rooming house with 14 rental units, five fire escapes and 'exit' signs everywhere. It was filled with mahogany and oak paneling, drop dead gorgeous. We paid full price, with the condition that the exit signs and the fire escapes had to be removed. We moved in the last day of school, with the boys on the top floor and in the playrooms in the basement."

Scenes from early Crawford family life in their home at 629 Humboldt St. Center photo shows Dana with sons, left to right, Tom, Peter, Duke and Jack, in 1961.

The house was perfect for the growing family, even idyllic in some ways. Not only did each boy have his own bedroom but they all were on the third floor, away from their parents on the second floor. Rounding out the perfect new home was Blaze, a golden retriever, which John's mother had won as a six-month-old puppy in a bingo game in Tulsa.

John and Dana adored the house, with its large shade tree in the backyard, meandering garden, comfortable patio and large carriage house back by the alley. "John loved it," Dana said. "In the garden, he planted trees, bushes, flowers, everything. And he loved the patio. I think that in every man's life, there must be a patio."

685 EMERSON STREET

The house was built in 1900 for Harry Crowe James, whose wealth came from gold and silver mining "by tripping over the right rock," as legend had it. He was an early supporter of the fledgling Colorado Museum of Natural History, now the Denver Museum of Nature & Science, in City Park. The Emerson Street house was designed by George Bettcher, who also designed the Denver Turnverein, a German dance hall, and the Rossonian Hotel in Five Points. When the house was built, the sidewalks down to 6th Avenue were made of wood.

Neighborhood lore had the newspaper boy asking Mr. James if he might loan him enough money for college tuition, promising Mr. James that he would pay it all back. James agreed and sent the boy to college. The newspaper boy, Thomas Hornsby Ferril, not only paid the money back but made the most of his education, eventually being named Poet Laureate of Colorado.

The enormous family home which the Crawfords moved into in 1967, on the southwest corner of 7th Avenue and Emerson Street. The four Crawford boys came of age in the 10,000 square-foot former rooming house.

Courtesy, © James O. Milmoe

When the Crawfords moved into 685 Emerson, everything had been organized and packed so well that the move took only one day. "By 6:30 that night, every piece of china and silver had been unpacked. It was the most orderly house move we had ever made," Dana said. "Evie and Tom Phoenix and Marge and Bob Priester brought us dinner that night which turned into a party with martinis that went way too late."

Summer vacation for the four boys started the next morning. John loved the outdoors and encouraged his sons to become active by teaching them to ski and taking them camping and on rafting trips down rivers on the Western Slope. The family belonged to the Arapahoe Tennis Club at East Quincy Avenue and Dahlia Street, about 10 miles away.

"We rode bikes out there, or got rides (mostly from Dana)," said Duke, the youngest son. "There were fireworks on July 4th. We got interested in swimming and diving and great tans."

"The boys were just wild, high energy. They fought with one another, Duke and Tom especially," said Dana. "John and I would take the boys out into the back yard and let them go at each other.

I was constantly trying to learn the psychology of what to do with them."

The family had become the closest of friends with the Congdons, who had three daughters about the same ages as the Crawford boys. "We were so close that if anything happened to either set of parents, we'd go to the other family," said Duke. "They were our true godparents."

Tragically, the Congdons lost their daughter Natasha at 17, when she slipped and fell while hiking on a school trip in the Wet Mountains of the Sangre de Christo range in southern Colorado. "Tasha" died on Oct. 8, 1978, Duke's 18th birthday. In her memory, the Crawfords planted a tree in their backyard. Jack Crawford later would name his second daughter after her.

The neighborhood was crowded with kids of all ages. Across Emerson, the Monleys had 12 kids; the Jacksons to the south of them had four boys; and across the alley were Kay and Ralph Schomp, the automobile dealer, and their six daughters. Alan Prendergast, who would make his name writing for Westword, grew up in the 700 block of Emerson, while Bridget and Gurnee Munn grew up with their mother Peggy just to the south of the Crawfords.

*Dana and John Crawford at the height of their creativity and productivity
in transforming Larimer Square into a nationally recognized gathering
place. Their vision and tenacity made them some of the earliest leaders in the
nation of historic preservation—of giving new economic life to notable older
buildings. They also were raising a family of four young boys born within
five years of each other.*

"It was a kids' paradise," said Caroline Schomp, who said her father refused to join the Denver Country Club because of the cost and instead built a swimming pool in their backyard. He also bought a large trampoline, which was a neighborhood favorite. Peter Crawford once broke his arm on the trampoline and went two weeks thinking it was just sore before he learned it was broken.

"Back then, we rode bikes from morning till dinner," Caroline said. "We'd ride out to Fairmount Cemetery or over to Stapleton Airport."

Meg Schomp, the youngest of the six Schomp girls, remembered listening to Carole King's "Tapestry" album with Jack in his basement. "When we graduated from (East) high school, Dana let us throw a very fancy dress-up party in her house, with white linens, crystal and china," said Meg. "What I remember most is Jack and his friends brought cigarillos to it. They were trying to learn to smoke, and got very sick, green in the face."

Dana's reputation as a tough negotiator and landlady in Larimer Square followed her home to the neighborhood. Federal Judge John Kane, who lived in the 700 block of Emerson Street, recalled a neighborhood meeting to discuss an upcoming large gathering of members of a national organization that was headquartered at East 7th Avenue and Ogden Street, one block away. Neighbors were fearful of parking problems, crowds, noise and other imagined dangers. Various remedies were being suggested when one neighbor stood up and said, "Why don't we ask Dana Crawford to deal with them?" Another neighbor, a psychologist, stood up and said, "No, we just want to stop them. We don't want to kill them."

"Why don't we ask Dana Crawford to deal with them?" Another neighbor, a psychologist, stood up and said, "No, we just want to stop them. We don't want to kill them."

The two Munn children were slightly older. "Bridget was 16 when I was 9," recalled Duke. "She already had a bottom and boobs, which was fascinating to me." Dana remembers Duke being more than fascinated with Bridget.

The Crawford boys all went to Dora Moore Elementary School at 8th Avenue and Downing Street, then to Morey Middle School at 14th and Emerson. By 10th grade, each boy would leave home to study at the Phillips Academy boarding school in Andover, Massachusetts, a three-generation tradition among Crawford men.

As the four Crawford boys matured into adulthood, their personalities emerged. Jack was considered to be the smartest of the four. Tom was intellectual and quiet, Peter was very outdoorsy and interested in health, while Duke "was the most handsome of all."

"Holidays were very big for us," said Dana. "One Christmas, there were no presents for me under the tree. The boys sat me down in the middle of the living room floor and blindfolded me. When they took it off, I was surrounded by four cases of wine with every bottle different. They had been selected by John. The idea was to have a big tasting because we loved wine so much.

"Well, the Crawford boys were old enough where we could include them in the tastings, or so we thought. By the second or third tasting, they all got tipsy and that turned into revelations by them of all the naughty things they had been doing, like throwing eggs at Peggy Munn's house, smoking pot or walking down the alley with a BB gun shooting out windows."

John Crawford plays with son Peter, Christmas morning, 1961.

Courtesy Crawford Collection

Into the cacophony of 685 Emerson Street came Michael Touff, a quiet, somewhat shy man who had just finished his studies at Harvard, the London School of Economics and the University of Michigan law school. He was looking to start his career as a lawyer and his mother convinced Dana to rent him the carriage house in back. He was roughly halfway in age between Dana and her oldest son, Jack.

"I'd be in the kitchen with the boys telling me their wildest dreams of what they wanted to do, like riding freight trains or hitch-hiking to Mexico," Dana said. "Michael would come in after work, open a beer and listen to them. He'd start talking and eventually calm them down by telling them about all the dangers of what they wanted to do. It was marvelous. He had a big influence on them."

When Jack got married, he was afraid to pick one of his brothers over the others to be his best man. So Michael Touff did the honors in a large ceremony at St. John's Episcopal Church.

Jack was an exceptional student who studied at Brown University, then received a master's degree in finance from the London School of Economics, through some influence from Touff. Tom was also a good student who went to New York University, then received a Ph.D. from Teachers College at Columbia University and is now a psychologist in New York. Peter was the only Crawford boy who didn't adapt to the formalities of Andover, so he transferred his junior year to Colorado Rocky Mountain School in Carbondale, where Natasha Congdon was enrolled when she died. Peter received a degree in holistic medicine from Metropolitan State College in Denver. Duke graduated from Andover and received a bachelor's degree in fine art from the Rhode Island School of Design, after spending his senior year studying in Rome.

Dana continued to hone her social skills and grow her network of friends and acquaintances and business connections. The house was perfect for entertaining.

David French, the developer, bought a house across from the Crawfords, at 680 Emerson and attended many of Dana's dinner parties. "In that big dining room, she'd have 20 people," he said. "It was always such an eclectic group of people, not just real estate people but artists, politicians, what not." Interior designers Marc Roth and Jim Pfister, both openly gay which was a rarity at the time, did design work for her, so she invited them.

"They were long evenings, not just cocktails but full dinners," said French. "The conversations were marvelous and there was never too much wine. The best invitation you could get was to one of Dana's dinner parties, which have become an obsolete art."

She'd throw parties for all sorts of reasons—Halloween, Mardi Gras, July 4th, costume parties, toga parties. Curt Fentress, the architect who designed Denver International Airport, the convention center and Sports Authority Field (Broncos stadium), was a neighbor of the Crawfords and attended some of the parties. "I was always amazed. Some of these parties would go on until 4 in the morning, people coming and going. I always wondered if they had any locks on the doors," he said.

Duke recalled how he and his brothers would sneak halfway down the stairway to spy on their parents' parties. "They would have raucous laughter attacks while drinking. We were little kids sitting on the stairs, listening to them sing bawdy songs," he said.

Dana wasn't the only member of the crowd to throw parties. Bill Saslow, one of the earliest developers in LoDo, owned a row of townhomes at 18th and Blake. An avid tennis player, Saslow built a tennis court in the back, and then added a small pool. It was a dicey neighborhood for such amenities. He named it the Blake Street Bath and Racquet Club, which is still there.

"Almost every Saturday, Dick and Maddie Gibson and John and Dana would come with their kids to the Blake Street club," Saslow said. "We'd play doubles, then have brunch around the pool. We threw a surprise party for Dana's 46th birthday. My wife, Diane, and I told Dana and John to come over for a drink, then we'd go out for dinner. When they got there, 60 to 80 people were hiding outside. We had a fabulous surprise party, which got a bit raunchy when five women stripped naked and jumped into the pool."

Tennis doubles at the Blake Street Bath and Racquet Club. Left to right, Ted Shugrue, Fredye Wright Gross, Maddie Gibson and John Crawford.

John and the young boys
on the cover of *The Denver Post's Contemporary Magazine, June 17, 1962.*

Dana seemed to be working day and night, totally committed to making Larimer Square as good as it could be. John worked hard as well, but didn't have Dana's depth of commitment. He accomplished much, particularly in dealing with architects, contractors, city inspectors, bankers and bookkeeping. He assisted in selecting tenants, sometimes taking them out to dinner with Dana. He was a valuable cog in the machinery. But he also liked to have a cocktail toward the end of the day, sometimes two or more. He always drank Old Overholt Kentucky rye whiskey, which had been very popular with soldiers in World War II as "medicinal". Some who don't care for it refer to it as "Old Overalls."

"Being so detail oriented as I am, hung up on wanting everything right from my perspective, I'm sure it was difficult for everybody," Dana said. "We were always struggling with the financing. Sometimes we would take those discussions home, which wasn't a good idea. We wouldn't fight. We'd disagree on priorities but we'd get it worked out. We could talk well.

> **"We had a lot of parties. I guess as party people we both drank a lot. It's challenging when a couple lives and works together."**

John was very gregarious with a terrific sense of fun and humor. He and his close friend Tommy Phoenix started a tradition of eating dinner every Dec. 7th in a Japanese restaurant to celebrate the victory over the Japanese after their attack on Pearl Harbor in 1941.

"If you go back through the newspaper clippings, John was very, very involved," Dana said. "People always give me the credit but he was there. He was onboard when we opened the Oxford Hotel. He mostly listened to me worry, but he brought in some of the investors."

His sons loved him dearly and thoroughly enjoyed their outdoor adventures in the mountains. But at home, he could drift away, sometimes on the patio, sometimes in front of the television, sometimes anywhere.

John had trouble disciplining his kids; it wasn't his style and he'd leave it up to Dana. He was a typical father of the 1960s…never gave a baby its bottle, never went to the grocery store, never charbroiled a steak, never even boiled water. "There were things he did and things he didn't do," Dana said. "This was standard for guys that age."

John in a pensive moment.

He liked television in general and would become addicted to sports programs, sometimes curled up in the chair, smoking heavily, alone in another world.

In a letter to her father on his 80th birthday in 1982, Dana wrote that John is "still sometimes great, sometimes not." He and Dana's father had a small falling out, about which Dana advised her father to not overreact and just go on.

"It seems to me that is what life is about—just go on," she wrote.

Friends remarked that both John and Dana seemed to mellow as parents with each new kid coming up, that they had been much tougher on Jack than they'd been on Duke.

Jack was very aware of it. After graduating from Brown University, he agonized about whether he should go to the London School of Economics. He went, and in his first letter home from London, he wrote that he wondered if his parents had even noticed how hard it had been for him to decide.

In another letter from London, Jack wrote that he understood his mother better than he understood his father, but resented her silent treatment of him, which came across as "a coolly unspoken but powerful expectation about what I should be doing." His father's distance was more acute, and he wrote: "There were times when I wished I could hash my uncertainties out with both of you. But, Dad, I never really have any idea of what's honestly going through your mind."

Duke becomes pensive talking about his dad. "I remember that the 1970s were torture for my mother and father," he said. "My father played a big role. Dana was hot; she was ferocious. My father called himself the blocking back and my mother was the running back."

"He was the sweetest guy," Duke said. "He loved to party, loved to flirt with the ladies but always in a non-threatening way. He'd call them Miss Sarah or Miss Jenny or Miss Something. He never strayed away from mom, never veered—zero."

John had been married once before Dana, briefly and unhappily.

Duke said his uncle, John's brother, told him there had been no such thing as PTSD among soldiers in World War II; that Gen. Patton "would whup you in the head if he heard you complain." The same had been true for their father, Duke's grandfather, who had fought hand-to-hand in World War I. Drinking was a common outlet, or release, among soldiers back then. "Hell yes, I think this was a big factor in his (John's) drinking. It was also habitual for him. He had very strong habits. But his drinking sure fueled a lot of fun. So many parties, always full of laughter."

In social and drinking situations, John was funny and warm and connected. Once the fun started, he would have trouble slowing down or stopping his drinking, frequently to the point where he had to be driven home by a friend.

Managing the Square didn't get easier as the business matured. In some ways, it became more difficult. The demands and duties changed but the drain on Dana and John was constant. By the 1980s, John's drinking was affecting his marriage, according to friends. He was not directly involved in Dana's decision to invest in the Oxford Hotel, although they invested their money together in the hotel. John did some work for Dana on the Oxford, primarily raising funds.

David French, a neighbor on Emerson and a tenant in Larimer Square, said, "I knew that John Crawford had a drinking problem but I never paid much attention to it. They raised some really good kids."

John's closest male friend was Tom Congdon, one of the original investors in Larimer Square. "When Dana bought into the Oxford Hotel, John wasn't involved. I think he felt very alone then, which might have added to his drinking."

Jill Crow, an arts philanthropist, became close friends with the Crawfords. "I loved John, even when he was drunk. He was always delightful and charming. Inside Café Promenade, I remember John more than Dana," she said.

The last photo taken of John W. R. Crawford III
before his death of a heart attack in October 1985.

On a Tuesday evening, Oct. 29, 1985, John and two close friends, noted sculptor Fred Myers and Constance Mortell, went downstairs into the Café Promenade for drinks. Dana was in Kansas visiting her father, who had become very sick.

"We had a great evening, a typical evening in Café Promenade. We toasted Dana and kept drinking," Constance said.

When they left, John walked west across Larimer Street down into a small, basement-level walkway that led to the alley and parking lot on Market Street. Mid-stride, he suffered a massive heart attack and dropped to the sidewalk. A shop owner called an ambulance, which arrived quickly and took him the short distance up Speer Boulevard to Denver General Hospital. But the ambulance crew had been unable to revive him. He was dead on arrival.

Constance and Fred rushed to the hospital. "We went to Denver General but John was dead, he'd died within half an hour of the heart attack," said Constance. "We saw his body, which was changing as the life force was leaving him. The color changes. Fred and I were dumbfounded. It took your breath away that you'd been with somebody and then they're gone. John was my first friend to die. We had just toasted Dana."

Fred Myers called Dana in Salina and told her. She talked to her sons—Jack was in Washington, D.C., Duke and Tom were in New York and Peter was in Denver. She flew back to Denver the next day, and was met at Stapleton Airport by Duke, Tom, and Barbara and Bill Hornby.

"I didn't get home until mid-afternoon," said Dana. "I walked into the house and it was filled with flowers. Constance had placed gigantic groups of flowers in every room. It was totally amazing."

Constance said she didn't know what to do. "I decided to get as many flowers as I could; it was an intuitive reaction. That house was gorgeous but it needed some life in it to greet her; that's why I did the flowers. I got dozens and dozens and dozens. I had to call a number of florists. We had them on the steps, in the house, all around so she'd have something to cheer her up or help her feel a little better. I wanted to ease the pain. I was in pain."

Duke had just moved to New York City to work as an artist. "I saw Dad shortly before he died. He didn't fill out his coat like he used to," he said. "Dad smoked Marlboros, a pack to a pack-and-a-half a day, and always thought he'd die at 55, like his father did. (John was 63.) That was my worst day, to lose a parent. Dana was destroyed."

John was cremated and his ashes placed in a crypt under the All Souls' Walk on the east side of St. John's Cathedral in Denver. Dana has reserved the space next to him.

The funeral service in St. John's was remarkable for the number of people who attended.

Tom Congdon, John's closest friend, wrote the eulogy and recited it to the gathering.

"...One doesn't have to search far for words to describe him. John Crawford was a gentleman. In fact, he kept close at hand for most of his life a definition of a gentleman. I believe he also drilled this into his sons as they grew up."

He then quoted from John's copy of Ralph Waldo Emerson's essay Manners. "...The word (gentleman) denotes good nature or benevolence; manhood first, and then gentleness."

Congdon continued: "...No one ever questioned John's manliness—particularly if you saw him take the ski mountain in one straight shot. But it was for his gentleness that we all loved John. He was a hard worker, modest, self-effacing—but above all—he was a gentleman..."

Dana and John celebrate their 25th wedding anniversary in New York City on October 12, 1980, with their sons, left to right, Peter, Tom, Jack and Duke.

Congdon later remarked that Dana suffered a great deal after John's death.

"His wake was the best," said Bruce Ducker, the lawyer/tenant/novelist in Larimer Square. "There were so many wonderful stories about him, like a purge. All kinds of people talked about John. When I was leaving, Mary Hoagland wrapped her arm inside mine and said, 'Isn't this a wonderful city?' John had many friends, although I think most of them were Dana's."

John Crawford's funeral was Nov. 1, 1985. The following week, Dana was still reeling when she decided to take some of the flowers over to Denver General Hospital for the patients to enjoy. The phone rang. It was Nov. 9, and Dana's father had just died. Within two weeks, she had lost two of the most meaningful men in her life.

Dale Carlin Hudkins had been a heavy smoker, 4-5 packs a day, for a substantial part of his life but lived to 83. He'd been sick for several months and fortunately, Dana had taken the time to visit him before he died. His only survivors were Dana and her four sons.

"Dana was destroyed," said Duke. "She's very sensitive. She was so overwhelmed by the two deaths that she made us fly in two separate planes to Salina so that the family wouldn't be wiped out in a crash. I flew with Jack.

"After we all got back, we got out the Old Overholt and toasted Dad, except for Peter who hated drinking."

Dana never dated after John's death, preferring to work, to travel and spend time with friends. "I guess I'm just a traditional one-man woman," she said much later. John Eaton, her beau in high school who also lived in Denver, began taking her out for occasional dinners when they had reached their 80s. But Dana said it never amounted to anything, that Eaton had become too conservative for her in his old age.

Dana's resiliency took over. She sold Larimer Square, began focusing more on preservation issues nationally and started converting two abandoned warehouses into Denver's first lofts. She lived alone in the Emerson Street house for some time after John's death, and later took in some college students as boarders.

In early 1991, Jack Crawford, the eldest son, and his wife Madeline, purchased an enormous, beautifully restored Italianate house at 2900 Champa Street. It was 6,000 square feet above ground, had eight wood-burning fireplaces and had been extensively refurbished by its previous owners. Door frames and wood moldings had been stripped to bare wood, then refinished. Vincent Scully, the preeminent architectural critic at Yale University, visited the house and called it one of the best examples of Italianate design in the United States, according to the Crawfords.

No sooner had Jack and Madeline purchased the house than Dana proposed a swap—she would take over Champa Street and Jack and Madeline, who were expecting their first child, would have Emerson Street. They made the swap primarily to avoid taxes and Jack and Madeline moved into Emerson without having spent a single night in the Champa Street house. Dana would continue the tradition of parties at the Champa location, but on a diminished scale.

The Denver Post had an excellent restaurant and wine critic, Bill St. John, who was so fastidious about his restored Mercedes Benz that he'd wipe his fingerprints off the

> "I guess I'm just a traditional one-man woman"

Courtesy, © James O. Milmoe

The elaborately restored Italianate Renaissance house at 2900 Champa St., which Jack purchased, then swapped with his mother for the 685 Emerson St. house.

door handle after locking it. "When I lived on Champa Street, I got a letter from Bill St. John, who wrote that after 22 years of marriage, he had come out of the closet as a gay man, with no place to live," said Dana. "I said he could live in the attic apartment if he helped with the snow shoveling and cooking and would bring me wine. He accepted and lived a couple of years with me." Barbara Macfarlane, who later married Pete Marczyk and co-founded Marcyzk Fine Foods grocery stores, lived there as well, after St. John moved out and before she married Pete.

A while later, in 1995, she came down with a severe case of pneumonia, which put her into the intensive-care unit for a number of days. "I damn near died," was how she summed it up.

Youngest son Duke got back to Denver as quickly as he could, with Dana still hospitalized but out of intensive care. He rushed into the room to see his mother lying motionless. "She was in bed with tubes coming out of her nose and mouth. One of her arms was taped to the gurney," he said. "She looked at me with these desperate eyes, tearing up, then motioning me to come close to her. I was afraid.

"I leaned over and she slapped me in the face. 'Don't take this too seriously,' she said with a laugh."

Once she was ready to leave the hospital, Dana felt more comfortable recuperating in the Oxford Hotel, with room service, so she stayed there 10 days. She remembers it was the same time Coors Field opened with the streets mobbed down below her window. Duke finally arrived, took her home and stayed with her for six weeks.

In 2008, Dana had another health scare that went from bad to worse. She went in for a checkup and doctors put a stent in one of her arteries because of her family history; her mother and grandmother had died of heart attacks. But shortly after the procedure, she started going downhill again. "My heart rate had dropped to 37," she said.

Back in the hospital, surgeons installed a pacemaker in the left side of her chest and accidentally sliced open her left lung during the procedure. It began to fill with blood and other fluid and she went "code blue" (requiring resuscitation) on the operating table, she recalled. The surgeons scrambled to sew up her lung and finish installing the pacemaker.

"They had put me under so I didn't know at all about the sliced lung," she said. "A lung thing can be horribly painful. But it was more traumatizing for the kids than for me."

Immediately, calls went out to Jack, who was in Europe; then Duke who was on a bicycle tour in Mexico; then Tom who was in New York. Peter was unreachable. With no family available, they called Jill Crow, Dana's close friend who came to the hospital immediately. Word spread quickly among her friends.

"Dana was so vulnerable, it was unimaginable," said Fabby Hillyard, another close friend of Dana's. "What an outpouring of concern that came from so many people, even some she had trampled on."

By the time Jack arrived in her hospital room, she had developed a staph infection and everybody was required to wear gowns, masks and gloves. The nurse told Jack that Dana couldn't talk because of a respirator tube, which was scheduled to be removed in 24 minutes. He walked over to Dana and took her hands in his.

"Jack explained that he couldn't talk to me but that he was holding my hands for another 24 minutes until they pulled out the respirator," Dana said. "Isn't that sweet, I thought. He's holding my hand for the rest of the time I have to live."

"So I'm now a computerized woman; my heart rate never goes below 60. My kids were fantastic, Duke took care of me and I'm fine," she said.

Dana got back to work as quickly as she could, and resumed her normal lifestyle of work, friends and dinner parties.

In the summer of 2011, Jock Bickert rented a villa in Tuscany for a month to celebrate his 80th birthday and his daughter's 40th, bringing along with them their entire family including grandkids. The villa had six bedrooms, six bathrooms, 8 acres, a garden and a pool. Jock also invited a number of friends, carefully scheduling their visits so that everyone would fit. Dana was invited to stay at the end of the month, to celebrate her 80th birthday.

In grand style, Dana invited Duke to drive her around Italy for about a week before arriving in Tuscany for the party. As they flew into Rome, Duke announced to Dana he had invited his Belgian girlfriend, Anna, to join them. Not surprised, Dana got into the car and the three of them took off across Italy.

When they arrived in Tuscany, the villa was bursting with 17 people, including Tom and Noe Congdon, two of Dana's closest friends. Bickert did the math and told Dana there was only one bedroom, with one bed, for the three of them. Anna and Dana discussed it at length, over wine, and decided they would share the bed. Duke would have to sleep on the tile floor or out in the hammock.

Dana's birthday dinner lasted four and a half hours, with Bickert's grandchildren doing all the serving. The party was a huge success. Dana, Anna and Duke left the next morning, drove to Bologna for a night, then back to Rome. They arrived in Rome late at night, too late to get a hotel room, Dana said. Energetically, she suggested they spend the rest of the night touring Rome, without the tourists, crowds and congestion that Rome is so well known for. Duke had lived in Rome for a year and he could be their tour guide.

Six hours later, they arrived at the airport, with an hour to kill. Dana, 80 years old and not concerned one whit about formality, got into the back seat, stuck her bare feet out the window and slept for an hour before the flight.

· LODO COMES ALIVE ·

"City leaders from all over the country have flocked to our historic doors to determine how we have accomplished so much in so little time," Dana, accepting the 1995 National Trust's highest award for her work in LoDo.

"The more I think about what I've been through, the more I don't know why anyone would want to be a developer," Dana, 20 years later.

John and Dana Crawford brought a new understanding and attitude to downtown Denver, one completely at odds with the "renewal" fever sweeping the nation in the 1960s and '70s, which held that old was bad and new was good. Demolish the old buildings and build new—with square corners of steel and drywall, said advocates of urban renewal. Against that current, the Crawfords, almost subconsciously, brought into Denver an attitude of urban "revival." Their work would transform Denver's thinking and direction for a half-century.

The revival approach to repairing the soul of a city would prove to be much more powerful, attractive and exciting than the renewal concept, with its bulldozer mentality, which caused immeasurable damage to downtown Denver.

Without realizing it, the Crawfords would become early leaders of a growing movement to honor and preserve many of the nation's sturdy and artistically designed structures. The Crawfords showed Denver a new appreciation for old buildings that could be reclaimed and renovated in new, pleasing and profitable ways. That revival attitude in Denver would spread slowly throughout the city, into the South Platte River Valley, up to Highland, out to Curtis Park and elsewhere, making Denver one of the most desirable places to live in the country.

"Larimer Square was a collection of old buildings," said Bill Mosher, president of the Downtown Denver Partnership for nearly 10 years and head of the International Downtown Association for a year. "Dana Crawford didn't preserve the past. She preserved the buildings of the past, the image of the past. But she took Larimer Square in a whole new direction. Dana understood how to preserve part of the past and move forward with that history.

"Today, Larimer Square is tied into the new economy. It's filled with young people; it's filled with empty nesters, with tourism and conventions. It's filled with people from all over the world who like to go there for its restaurants and coffee shops and stores. That's not what Larimer Street was back in the 1890s."

JANE JACOBS *THE DEATH AND LIFE OF GREAT AMERICAN CITIES*

Proponents of urban revival rarely if ever have the financial and political clout of their urban renewal counterparts. But advocates of historic preservation have champions like Jane Jacobs, author of the seminal 1961 book, *The Death and Life of Great American Cities*. In a David vs. Goliath mismatch, Jacobs, who favored neighborhoods and pedestrians, challenged New York master planner Robert Moses, who favored driving everywhere in cars, and to that end had designed the Cross Bronx Expressway. His next project would be a 10-lane, elevated expressway across lower Manhattan from the Holland Tunnel on the west side directly through Greenwich Village and Washington Square Park to the Williamsburg Bridge on the east side. Jacobs, who lived in Greenwich Village, and her followers spent 10 years fighting Moses and City Hall, eventually stopping the $100-million (in 1962 dollars) plan, which Moses callously referred to as "slum clearance."

In Denver, the area below Larimer Street down to the South Platte River had decayed during the 1930s and '40s, with little improvement to the area in the ensuing decades. In June 1965, just months after Larimer Square had been announced, 10 inches of rain fell within 24 hours, flooding the entire Central Platte Valley with water, mud, sewage and slime.

View of the flood along the South Platte River, Denver, Colorado; general view from a helicopter shows the railroad yards south of the 14th Street Viaduct, the Colorado and Southern Railway shops. The Atchison, Topeka and Santa Fe and Denver & Rio Grande Western main lines curve south at top of photo.

Downtown Denver also had suffered from neglect since before the Depression. For nearly three decades until the early 1950s, not a single building taller than four stories had been built in the city's central business district. William Zeckendorf's 24-story Mile High Center at 17th and Broadway, which opened in 1955, was the first new building constructed in downtown Denver since the end of World War I. Denver was losing much of its tax base to new suburbs with their tract housing and sprawling shopping centers. Most of Denver's leaders, bankers and planners were fearful for the city's future.

In the aftermath of World War II, the federal government began responding to these fears across the country by making large amounts of money available for new residential housing—aimed at replacing the slums with low-income housing and building new single family homes for returning veterans.

"It was a national trend, it was understandable," Dana said. "The post-war cities wanted to start over. There had been no new development except for the likes of Zeckendorf. All this new money would be a big shot in the arm."

In 1955, Denver's leaders formed the Conservation Redevelopment Board to deal first with residential slums, primarily because housing had become such an important issue with returning World War II veterans. The city's worst slum, "Frog Hollow" at 6th Avenue and the South Platte River, was destroyed and not replaced because of the new interstate highway that was being built through the valley. After 10 years of construction, Interstate 25, or "the Valley Highway," opened in 1958. Two other residential slums, Avondale near West Colfax Avenue and Federal Boulevard and Whittier, near 29th and Downing streets, were demolished but replaced with low-income housing.

By 1958, the redevelopment board had been restructured into the Denver Urban Renewal Commission, which later became the Denver Urban Renewal Authority (DURA). In 1963, DURA aimed its "renewal" philosophy at downtown Denver's Central Business District (CBD). After seemingly endless studies, meetings, delays and lawsuits, DURA announced it had targeted the lower end of the CBD for urban renewal. The Skyline Urban Renewal Project encompassed 27 blocks, or 113 acres, bounded by Cherry Creek on the south to 20th Avenue on the north, and from the alley between Market and Larimer streets east to Curtis Street. Owners and tenants would be uprooted, the buildings purchased with federal funds, then demolished. The authority believed that developers would rush in, purchase the empty lots and rebuild anew. Critics complained that DURA had no overall plan and no control over the replacement buildings, that they would be designed and built piecemeal by individual architects and developers with no consistency or control.

DURA and City Hall started a fierce PR campaign to convince taxpayers to approve the plan, which included raising the city's sales tax to 2 percent, with a portion of the tax money to be used for purchase and demolition of the targeted buildings. The Denver Post supported the plan, calling the existing buildings "undistinguished piles of old brick." Pocky Marranzino at the Rocky Mountain News urged citizens

Aerial view of downtown Denver parking lots created by the Denver Urban Renewal Authority's obsession of demolishing the business district's older buildings. The program, funded by taxpayers, was so misguided that developers had very little interest in redeveloping the blocks, leaving DURA no choice but to pave over the land as parking lots for more than 3,000 cars. Larimer Square is just out of the picture's lower right corner.

"to obliterate Skid Row, perform radical surgery to remove the cancer of blight and breathe new and productive life into the area." The Chamber of Commerce also supported the plan.

Voters approved it by a 2-1 margin in May 1967.

The Skyline renewal was the largest capital-improvement project in the history of Denver. It also proved to be one of the most disastrous, ill-conceived and poorly implemented civic-improvement programs in the city's history. Many of Denver's architectural gems, including the Tabor Block, the Daniels and Fisher Department Store and the Frontier Hotel, were pulverized and trucked away. The Denver Landmark Preservation Commission, founded in 1967, attempted to persuade DURA to save eight historic buildings. Only two of them were saved: the D&F Tower at 16th and Arapahoe streets, and the Denver City Cable Railway Building, now the Old Spaghetti Factory, at 18th and Lawrence streets. In the end, so many buildings were leveled with such limited interest from developers to buy the land that DURA was forced to pave over much of its destruction, creating parking lots for more than 3,000 cars.

It seemed that almost everything that could go wrong did so. The first building to be demolished, the 8-story Cooper Building at 17th and Curtis streets, was dynamited at 7 a.m., April 5, 1970. A brave Denver police officer averted disaster after spotting a derelict near the building just seconds before ignition. The cop sprinted over, collared the wino and dragged him to safety as the roar of the dynamite thrilled the sizeable crowd gathered to watch. Eight seconds later, the 80-foot building was a pile of dusty rubble.

Denver Public Library, Western History Department, X-24928

The Cooper Building, at 17th and Curtis streets, was the first building to be demolished by DURA as part of its Skyline renewal project in April 1970. A quick-witted policeman spotted a bum near the building and rushed him to safety just moments before the building fell.

After the ominous start, developers soon were accusing DURA of playing favorites; adjacent parcels of land were being sold for very different prices; designs were scuttled; and developers couldn't get financing. Then things got worse. The economy slowed as a recession hit in 1974-75, driving commercial interest rates to 12% and homebuyers' rates as high as 16%. Construction came to a standstill.

In the early 1980s, when a shale-oil boom was expected, overly optimistic developers began building again. But by the late 1980s, the anticipated boom fizzled and turned to another bust. Skyscrapers, like the brand-new 56-story Republic Plaza, stood nearly empty and became known as "see through" buildings. Not long after the 16th Street pedestrian mall opened, people joked that downtown Denver was so deserted after 5 p.m. that they could roll a bowling ball down the mall and not hit a single pedestrian.

> **"The quality of the buildings being destroyed was unbelievable,"** said developer Bill Saslow. **"Skyline was one of the worst urban renewal projects in the country. Major subsidies were going to horrible buildings designed by second- and third-rate architects. Some buildings had no street level activity."**

So much for the "renewal" approach.

Dana Crawford's "revival" approach in Larimer Square ushered in a new attitude of renovating old buildings and giving them a new purpose, with much different results. It was a foreign concept to members of the Denver Urban Renewal Authority, and it conflicted with their goals. Authority members believed in their supreme authority to demolish buildings in order to cleanse an impoverished area. The Authority basked in the support of the city's leaders, the business community and the taxpayers, who had voted for a sales-tax increase to fund this invasion and occupation. The Authority had the belief it was on a noble mission that no one could stop.

No one, that is, except a proper young woman driving a "puke green" Ford convertible down Skid Row, looking for a "gathering place" for the city.

No sooner had Dana set her sights on the 1400 block of Larimer Street than DURA released a statement calling Larimer Street part of "the most deteriorated portion of downtown Denver." The Skyline District map marked both sides of Larimer Street from 14th to 19th streets for demolition.

Dana was undaunted and began making her move, knowing full well she would have to battle not just an "agency" but an "authority" with eminent domain power in order to save the block. She never was forced to lie down in front of the bulldozers, as legend has it. But she would have to rely on her brains, her wit and her fearlessness—everything she had—to keep those wobbly buildings away from the wrecking ball.

"DURA was afraid of Larimer Square," she said. "If it was successful, it might stop their plan. They wanted to wipe out everything."

Dana believed that the key to her success would be to make the Square economically viable as quickly as possible, then argue with the city that it was generating new taxes, more jobs and giving citizens a new place to enjoy themselves. To do that, she had one big advantage: the authority was notoriously slow to make decisions because of endless meetings, studies, consulting of experts and bureaucratic plodding. That would give her time to get Larimer Square in operation and, hopefully, begin drawing crowds and making money.

By the time Your Father's Mustache opened in December 1965, DURA still hadn't made any progress. The Crawfords continued to hustle to complete as many renovations as possible and get as many spaces leased as they could. Dana also used her substantial public relations skills to gain a tactical advantage by getting Mayor Tom Currigan and much of City Council to publicly support her project. She also generated extensive media coverage of her project.

As renovations proceeded on the east side of the 1400 block of Larimer, DURA quietly re-drew its map and ran the Skyline district's southwestern boundary down the center of Larimer Street. DURA, in effect, conceded the east side of the street to the Crawfords but wanted to take the buildings on the west side through eminent domain and demolish them. The Crawfords said no, then fought a long battle, running up substantial legal bills. DURA offered a compromise, a "development agreement" that would keep the west-side buildings intact if the Crawfords agreed to give DURA total control over the renovations and operations of the buildings.

> How little DURA understood its opponent. Nothing could infuriate Dana more than someone wanting to take control of her project. "They wanted to be in charge of every little detail, down to signs and paint. They wanted to control everything," she said. "That was impossible. We spent a lot of money in legal fees fighting them and we finally rolled over them."

Exactly one year after Your Father's Mustache opened in Larimer Square, DURA capitulated. Consultant Robert DeVoy went on record in December 1966, saying, "Larimer Square should be left alone as its future is favorable." By the time the Skyline plan went before the voters in May 1967, DURA had thrown in the towel, reclassifying Larimer Square as a "rehabilitation area" and no longer targeted for demolition.

Exempting Larimer Square irritated a number of less savvy building owners, particularly those who owned some of the 65 liquor stores and bars in the Skyline district that were being forced to shut down so their buildings could be demolished. City Councilman Robert Keating told the Denver Post that Larimer Square was being excluded from the district "because of silk stocking pressure."

Once Dana felt secure that DURA was not going to bulldoze Larimer Square, she reversed her earlier stance and publicly supported the rest of DURA's plans for the Skyline District. "It was going to be really good for the city, and for Larimer Square," she recalled, without a hint of irony or hypocrisy.

Other property owners welcomed DURA's plan as an opportunity to move their businesses out of what had become Skid Row. They included the Cook and Gart families, which owned large sporting goods stores respectively at 1601 and 1643 Larimer Street. They saw DURA's eminent domain powers as their chance to get rid of their buildings, which were nearly impossible to sell. So they supported the Skyline plan, and Dana, having saved her own project, joined them.

"Obviously, I had to fight urban renewal for Larimer Square. But the area was considered a blight because of the demographics there. Nobody else gave a damn about the buildings," she said.

The concept of preserving old buildings would grow rapidly across the country. In 1965, New York City passed its Landmarks Law, creating the Landmarks Preservation Commission after a bitter fight failed to save Penn Station from the wrecking ball the year before. In 1966, Congress passed the National Historic Preservation Act, which spurred Denver to pass its own landmark Preservation Ordinance in 1967. By then, Dana had become thoroughly familiar with the philosophy of "preservation" and had begun to gather an army of like-minded preservationists. They lost their first real test when they failed to keep the exceptional 42-room Moffat Mansion at East 8th Avenue and Grant Street from being demolished. That landmark was replaced by a modest, forgettable office building.

Their next significant engagement would be to save the historically significant home of Molly Brown, who survived the sinking of Titanic. To bolster their strength, Dana and others formed Historic Denver Inc. in 1970. The turning point came when Historic Denver and other preservationists saved the house, at 1340 Pennsylvania St., from demolition, a pivotal moment in the movement to save significant architectural structures in Denver. The house was listed on the National Register of Historic Places in 1972. It was turned into a museum and has become one of the city's more popular tourist spots.

With Dana's influence locally, the Denver City Council in July 1971 voted to name Larimer Square as the city's first historic district. With her influence nationally, Larimer Square was placed on the National Register of Historic Places in May 1973.

The magnificent, 42-room Moffat Mansion at 8th and Grant was demolished in the late 1960s to make room for an undistinguished, featureless office building. The loss of this iconic mansion was particularly painful for the growing preservation community, showing that the recently enacted Landmark Preservation Commission needed strengthening.

As DURA and its demolition crews concentrated on the central business district east and north of Larimer Square, the area to the west, in what is referred to today as LoDo, remained a gritty warehouse district for at least another decade. Larimer Square's success in bringing customers to the area day and night helped attract development on adjacent blocks, such as Writer Square and the 1400 block of Market Street. But it wouldn't be until 1990 when the economy improved before the rest of LoDo, with its solid brick structures, would be "discovered" for loft conversions, nightclubs and restaurants.

"Everybody in the development business was going out to the suburbs,"
Dana said. "Infill wasn't even a word yet."

Gretchen Bunn was one of the first people to move into LoDo when she and her husband, Ken, bought a two-story building in the 1500 block of Wazee Street in 1972. They paid $55,000 for a 6,200 square-foot building that had an elevator and another 3,000 square feet in the basement.

"The area was seedy, it was Skid Row with lots of bums and homeless men," Gretchen said. "The only businesses were the Wazee Supper Club (at 15th and Wazee streets), Rockmount Ranch Wear (16th and Wazee) and the Oxford Hotel (17th and Wazee), which had bare light bulbs in the rooms."

In 1981, nine years after she had moved in, Gretchen was stopped by police for prostitution one Sunday morning. She had run in her bathrobe down a block to the Oxford Hotel to buy a newspaper when the cops grabbed her. She told them what she was doing and they replied, "No one lives down here." They let her go.

Slowly Dana's pioneering spirit and her unexpected success with Larimer Square began to attract some of the more adventurous entrepreneurs to the area. Allan Reiver acquired four buildings in the 1500 block of Market Street, moved into one and used the other three to store architectural antiques he was gathering from the buildings about to be demolished.

Soon, Reiver teamed with Bill Saslow, who, with four Ivy League degrees (psychology, architecture, urban design and an MBA), was working for Billy White's Great Western United Corp, and architect Peter Dominick Jr., a classmate of Saslow who was working for William Muchow designing buildings in the new Auraria campus, which opened in 1969. Saslow and his wife, Diane, had moved into the recently built Brooks Tower at 15th and Curtis streets, the first multi-family residential property in downtown Denver.

"The Wazee Three"— Allan Reiver, Bill Saslow, Peter Dominick, Jr.

The three men, dubbed "The Wazee Three," began scouring LoDo for buildings that could be redeveloped. The trio's first purchase, in 1972, was the Elephant Corral building at 1444 Wazee, where the large courtyard was being used to sell Christmas trees. They bought a number of properties on Wazee and Market streets, including the John Deere building at 15th and Wazee, and a string of townhomes at 18th and Blake streets, later converted into the Blake Street Bath and Racquet Club.

> **"It was very difficult for us to pull this off; we were following Dana's work," Saslow said. "Dana broke the barriers. It is incalculable what she brought to this city. She was a very ballsy woman."**

The Wazee Three, along with Dana and others, convinced the city in 1974 to change the zoning for a 20-block area between Larimer Square and Union Station to B-7. That area makes up LoDo today. B-7 zoning allowed the continuation of warehousing and light industrial uses, such as Rockmount Ranch Wear, but also allowed residential living and retail. It included significant incentives for rehabbing old buildings, which brought more developers into the area.

The area was beginning to attract some attention in the media, which always like to spot new trends and categorize them with nicknames or some easily remembered moniker. On Nov. 2, 1983, Denver Post columnist and man-about-town Dick Kreck wrote about lower downtown, putting his own shorthand to use by naming it "LoDo." The name stuck, as tight as gum on the sidewalk, and remains today. Dana disliked it and thought it was demeaning to the neighborhood.

The Oxford Hotel, at 17th and Wazee streets, is the oldest operating hotel in Denver. Designed by Frank Edbrooke and opened in 1890, catering to railroad travelers arriving in Union Station one block away. Dana invested in the hotel in 1980, went through Chapter 11 bankruptcy twice and still retains ownership with other investors.

In 1978, developer Charles Callaway put together a group of investors and bought the dilapidated Oxford Hotel on 17th Street for $500,000. The office vacancy rate in Denver in 1979 and 1980 was 0.5%, statistically as low as it can go. With the market that good, Callaway's investors wanted to turn the hotel into an office building, which wasn't Callaway's intention at all. He approached Dana, who put together another group of investors and bought Callaway's partners out. Without a crystal ball, the two had no way of knowing that they were embarking on a Herculean struggle that would last 10 years to save the old hotel.

OXFORD HOTEL

It was designed by Frank Edbrooke, who later would design the Denver Dry Goods building and the Brown Palace Hotel. The Oxford opened in 1890, making it Denver's oldest hotel still operating. Its original owner was Adolph Zang, son of the founder of Zang Brewery, the largest brewery west of the Mississippi until Prohibition shut it down. Zang also built the Lakeside Amusement Park and donated land for the Alamo Placita Park at Emerson Street and Speer Boulevard.

The Oxford catered to rail travelers coming into Union Station, a block away, and it flourished for decades. In 1912, the Oxford Annex was built to handle the overflow of guests. In 1933, its owners added the Cruise Room bar. During World War II, the bar was jammed with servicemen staying at the Oxford overnight before shipping out.

The Oxford Hotel's Art Deco Cruise Room bar, redesigned during the Great Depression to resemble a lounge from the Queen Mary. Individual panels celebrate various nations' popular terms for toasting friends before quaffing.

Photos: Tom Lundin, The Denver Eye

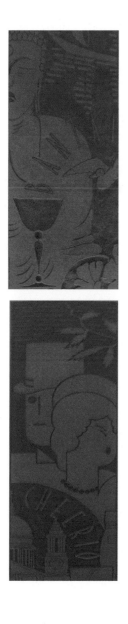

CRUISE ROOM

As Prohibition came to an end in 1933, architect Charles Jaka redesigned the Cruise Room cocktail lounge into an Art Deco version of a lounge that might be seen onboard the ocean liner Queen Mary. Laid out in the shape of a wine bottle, the elongated walls of this skinny lounge are lined with artist Alley Henson's hand-carved, bas-relief panels of people, in silhouette, celebrating various toasts around the world, from Cheers (British or Australian) to Salute or cin-cin (Italian) to Skål (Swedish) to Sante' (French). A panel showing Adolf Hitler and a swastika was removed during World War II, but can be seen in a photograph in the hallway.

Crawford and Callaway, in the early stages of their renovation of the Oxford, planned to move the Cruise Room to another location within the hotel. But the National Park Service denied their request because the bar, and nothing else in the hotel, had been placed on the National Register of Historic Places. It was a very rare occurrence to have one room inside a building declared a historic place. The Register lists the bar as one of the most outstanding examples of Art Deco Style.

The reddish-hued room is always brightly lit, usually full and cheerful, with remarkable bartenders pouring the best martinis in town.

> **"It was really, really difficult to get financing for a run-down hotel in an awful part of town,"** Dana said. **"I could give you 42 reasons why no one wanted to finance it. I met a traveling salesman for a high-end office furniture company. He was on such a tight budget that he'd stay in the Oxford, entertain his clients in the Brown Palace Hotel, then go back to the Oxford to sleep."**

In time, Dana and Callaway found financing and spent $12.5 million renovating the hotel, according to The Denver Post. The hotel reopened in June 1983 but its timing was all wrong. Denver was entering into a recession; the hoped-for oil boom was turning into a bust. The area around the hotel was still seedy, no one was traveling by train anymore and there was little reason for anyone to come to this part of downtown. Crawford and Callaway had hired a bumbling management company to run the hotel, which was struggling to stay half-full. A number of businessmen belonged to the Oxford Club, similar to men's clubs in London that allowed members to drink and dine on their signatures and not be billed until the end of the month. But the hotel's management, according to Dana, was so bad that it frequently forgot to bill club members for their charges. And when the bills did go out, the members would object, claiming they were higher than they should be. "We were in the food and booze business, and we lost a lot of money on food and booze," she said.

Faced with a miserable economy, a bad location and poor management, the hotel was forced to declare Chapter 11 bankruptcy not once, but twice. Dana recalls this period as the "Chapter 22" years.

"It's one of the reasons why I'm still here," she said, referring to protection offered by the court.

In 1986, she and Callaway were forced to partner with the Weyerhauser Corp. and Alexis Hotels for financial support and management. Callaway and Dana essentially lost control of the hotel and were relegated to roles as limited partners.

Meanwhile, a part-time telephone operator at the hotel, Christie Isenberg, went home and told her husband, Walter Isenberg, about the difficulties the hotel was having. He and his college classmate, Zack Neumeyer, had started Sage Hospitality in 1984 to manage hotels, most of them in bankruptcy or in the process of being repossessed during the savings and loan crisis. They were good at what they were doing; today Sage owns or manages more than 75 hotels, including The Crawford Hotel in Denver Union Station.

At that time of crisis in the 1980s, Walter, through his wife, met with Callaway and Dana in the Cruise Room bar to discuss a takeover of the Oxford. "I wrote on a cocktail napkin that Sage would bring in a net operating income of $700,000 or we'll leave," Isenberg said.

"Developer agreements in the hotel business were extremely hard to get out of," explained Dana. "Walter wrote it down on a napkin and said if he didn't make it, he'd rip it up. He said to us, 'I can assure you we're going to make money.'"

"The hotel had just gone into bankruptcy the second time," Isenberg recalled. "The debt was roughly $7.5 million with the note held by RTC (Resolution Trust Company). Dana and Charles went to Seattle and convinced Weyerhauser to sell the partnership back to them for $25,000. We terminated Alexis Hotels and Sage took over. It was our first equity investment."

To recapitalize the hotel out of bankruptcy, a number of local investors pitched in, including Sage, which invested $250,000; Diane Blackman, who invested $250,000; and Evan Makovsky, who loaned them $500,000. The Denver Employees Retirement Plan loaned them $4 million. Out of this reorganization, Dana and Charles each received 25% ownership; Sage and Blackman each had 10%; and small investors had the balance.

"Our critics said we were at the wrong end of town, there was no Coors baseball field, no Pepsi Center and lofts above the Wynkoop brewery were selling for $60,000," Isenberg said.

"We thought the hotel wasn't positioned correctly. The Brown Palace was the only 5-star hotel. So we decided we should be a neighborhood hotel, less formal than the Brown Palace. We'd be more Ralph Lauren; didn't matter if you had on jeans or a coat and tie.

"We cut expenses significantly and the income went up substantially. All of the unsecured creditors have been paid back in full. We're doing great now."

Now, room rates in the 80-room hotel average about $250 and occupancy averages more than 80 percent, he said. Sage and Dana are the hotel's general partners; Sage owns 60%, Dana about 20% and Callaway owns about 10%. Asked to describe the Oxford Hotel today, Isenberg called it "an authentic, historic, boutique Western hotel. We're smaller than the Brown Palace, more interesting, less formal and with more Western hospitality. And we have free coffee in the mornings."

The Oxford experience was a painful, powerful lesson for Dana. She shudders at the memory of those early days preserving and running the hotel. And it was during the worst of the mess that she lost her husband John. About the same time, she also sold off Larimer Square, which had been her anchor, her identity, her reason for getting up in the mornings. But typical of Dana, she sought help, she fought hard and gradually worked her way out of the hole into the current situation of owning a piece of one of Denver's grand hotels. Yet it left a lot of scars.

The Oxford Hotel

With the Oxford, Dana learned which fights to pick and which ones to let go of. She let Sage modernize the bathrooms, get rid of the iron bathtubs and put in flatscreen TVs. But she refused to replace the room keys with electronic cards. She argued that there is something about a real lock and key and a tassel that keeps the romance and history of the hotel. On that issue, a serious one because it involves security, Isenberg conceded to Dana's demand.

"She was right. We do a good job of security. Let's keep the keys, it's one of those charming little things at the Oxford," Isenberg said.

Isenberg has no regrets about joining Dana at the Oxford and didn't hesitate to join her more recently in helping renovate Union Station. Along the way, he's learned about her strengths and weaknesses.

"Dana's experiences with hotel operations didn't work well for her. Operations require process and discipline and organization. Those are not her core strengths," he said. "But she trusted us and allowed us to do what we do well. We were able to take advantage of her vision and creativity. Those are her strengths."

The Oxford was placed on the National Register of Historic Places in 1979 while Dana was serving on the board of directors of the National Trust for Historic Preservation.

Photos: Melanie Simonet

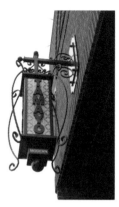

Larimer Street, Courtesy © James O. Milmoe

Dana's life continued to evolve in the late 1980s. Larimer Square had been sold, her headaches from the Oxford Hotel were being relieved by Sage Hospitality and she was beginning to travel extensively around the country as a consultant and board member of the National Trust. Always keeping an eye for business opportunities, she began noticing a trend in the older cities—New York, Boston and San Francisco — where developers were moving downtown into the old warehouse districts, buying up abandoned buildings and converting them into residential "lofts."

The term "loft" has its origin in sailing communities, where sailmakers would rent or buy enormous open spaces to "loft" large sections of canvas into custom-tailored sails. The term also became synonymous with attics or upper storage spaces, such as haylofts. Artists, notorious for finding cheap, rundown studio spaces, began renting the upper floors of industrial buildings, like in New York's Bowery and meatpacking district, Boston's waterfront district near South Station and San Francisco's market district. Dana watched these buildings being converted, some very nicely, into a new style of living.

She knew there was a latent interest among some people to live downtown; she had been asked many times in Larimer Square if there were residential spaces nearby. Her colleagues, once again, thought she was nuts. "No one will live in that area," they chided her. But she had seen it working in the larger, older cities. And Denver had some buildings that might work perfectly.

The savings and loan crisis was in full stride in the late 1980s, when nearly one-third of all "thrifts" were closed for bad loan portfolios from mortgages, car loans and personal loans. Across the country, the real estate market tanked. The Resolution Trust Corporation had been formed as a governmental agency responsible for selling foreclosed properties or those in bankruptcy. They were most commonly sold through auctions.

In 1988, Dana formed Urban Neighborhoods Inc. and began combing LoDo for abandoned warehouses in good shape. In 1989, she found a beauty at 1450 Wynkoop Street. The six-story, red-brick building had been designed by Frank Edbrooke, who also designed Dana's Oxford Hotel. Built in 1905 as a wholesale grocery warehouse designed

Denver Public Library, Western History Collection, X-20729

for heavy loads, the building had ceilings 13 to 18 feet high, supported by wooden beams 18 inches thick resting on top of posts that were as much as 12 inches thick.

Dana began negotiating to buy the building when unexpectedly it was bundled with others and sent to auction. Savvy about rigging auctions, Dana took two "ringers" with her and controlled the auction price, beating out fellow developer Jerry Glick, who later bought and redeveloped the Barteldes Seed Co. building at 1600 Wynkoop. Dana bought only the Edbrooke.

Once again, Dana's vision was beyond anything Denver had seen. This would be the first loft conversion in Denver, and the financing requirements she had to meet would have discouraged almost any other developer. She bought the building in 1989 with a group of investors that included Rike Wootten, an original investor in Larimer Square. She went to Central Bank and Trust, which had worked with her on Larimer Square, and asked for construction financing to convert the building. The bank had no confidence in the project but was familiar with Dana and her capabilities. So it agreed to give her construction financing provided she met three conditions: She had to pre-sell half of the 44 units; each buyer had to have pre-approved financing in writing; and the entire project had to be approved ahead of time by the Federal National Mortgage Association, or Fannie Mae. Those three conditions would kill most projects, particularly a warehouse project in a shabby area with no proven market for buyers.

> **Once again, Dana's vision was beyond anything Denver had seen. This would be the first loft conversion in Denver, and the financing requirements she had to meet would have discouraged almost any other developer.**

Dana pressed forward. She pre-sold half of the lofts but no Denver bank would give the buyers financing. So she went to Citicorp in San Francisco, which was familiar with lofts and actually believed, from its review of national studies, that loft buyers were good credit risks.

Dana and her assistant, Mona Kohler, flew to Dallas to visit Bill Peña in Fannie Mae's western regional office. He said: "Dana, we haven't approved a single purchase in the state of Colorado in three years. Why would we do this stupid building in this dumpy neighborhood?" In classic Dana Crawford style, she asked Peña if he had plans to come to Denver soon, which he did in three weeks. She asked him if he liked to drink martinis, which he did. "Well, Mr. Peña, we're going to have a

The 15th Street viaduct (now gone) begins at Wazee Street heading west past the Edbrooke Building, center. The elevated, concrete viaducts carried automobile traffic over the railroad tracks and the South Platte River to the west side of Denver.

party for you in that 'stupid old building' with all these buyers and then you can decide." Peña attended a "wonderful party" in the empty warehouse, and approved the project.

Dana renamed the building the "Edbrooke" and all 44 lofts sold out relatively quickly. Again, her vision was acute.

"Getting these lofts started was very important, especially for downtown," she said. "They were important because now people were living in LoDo 24 hours a day. It was important to have people call LoDo their 'home.' Now they would be watching and caring for the neighborhood."

Others agreed. "For those of us who grew up here, Denver was always a place of houses, yards and fences; not apartments and certainly not lofts," said Fabby Hillyard, who became director of the city's theaters and arenas and later executive director of the non-profit neighborhood association LoDo District Inc. "We were not so attuned to that kind of living. Dana was a beacon for what these non-traditional spaces could provide. She had a bigger idea of what the culture was all about."

The Acme Building at 14th and Wazee streets when Dana began to renovate it into residential lofts in 1992. The roadway directly in front of the building is westbound Speer Boulevard, which rises on an elevated viaduct over the South Platte River. Eastbound Speer is the elevated bridge to the rear of the Acme building. The bridge in the foreground is Wazee Street, traveling over Cherry Creek.

Right after her success with the Edbrooke, Dana in 1990 bought the Acme building on Wazee Street. At the time, westbound traffic on Speer Boulevard used the 14th Street viaduct, which passed on the north side of the Acme building, while eastbound traffic passed on the south side of the Acme. The viaducts were removed between 1988 and 1993. Speer Boulevard now uses one viaduct for both directions, south of the Acme.

This building, slightly smaller than the Edbrooke, was built in 1909 for the Brecht Candy company, which installed heavy machinery capable of producing up to 3 million pounds of candy each year, all made with Colorado sugar. The internal timber frame was similar to the Edbrooke's in size and strength. The Brecht company sold the building in 1952 to Acme Upholstery, which occupied it until 1968, hence the name change.

Dana pre-sold all 30 lofts designed for the Acme building, got a guaranteed maximum price from the contractor for renovations and still had to shop several banks before finding a construction loan.

**"Dana found the people to invest in non-traditional buildings, first in Larimer Square, then in the Oxford, the Edbrooke and the Acme,"
Hillyard said. "Eventually, LoDo started happening.
And soon the money began following Dana. In my opinion,
Dana was fully responsible for creating LoDo."**

With Dana proving that loft conversions had a large market of buyers, with rooftop lofts selling for as much as $750,000 in 1990, developers and their investors began buying everything they could find. Next door to the Acme building, Mickey Zeppelin purchased the Volker building, which was not only empty but also missing windows and by then home for dozens and dozens of pigeons. John Hickenlooper, a novice brewer who later became mayor of Denver then governor of Colorado, was building lofts above his Wynkoop Brewing Co. pub at 18th and Wynkoop streets.

Dana bought the Ice House diagonally across the corner from Hickenlooper and attempted to develop a design center for interior designers and decorators. It failed, in part, because of the traffic congestion that accompanied the opening of a new baseball stadium nearby. Developers Steve Owen and Don Betts bought the abandoned Streetcar Stables building at 1720 Wynkoop St. from the Resolution Trust

Corp. and, after figuring out how to rid the wood floors of the smell of horse urine, converted it into a mixed-use building of restaurants on the main floor and elegant lofts above. Owen bought the Ice House after Dana's aborted try and turned it into a mixed-use building with restaurants on the ground floor, a parking garage and residential lofts. Many other conversions followed, more restaurants and bars moved in and suddenly LoDo was the place to be.

Joyce Meskis, owner of the Tattered Cover bookstore and Fourth Story restaurant at 1st Ave. and Steele Street in Cherry Creek, had been presented with an enormous increase in rent by "The Evil Empire of the East," as she called a consortium of bankers who owned the building. So she and friend John Hickenlooper (she owned and lived in a loft in Hickenlooper's brewpub building) began looking in LoDo for another location for Tattered Cover.

"The properties in LoDo were so sad," Meskis said. "There were still more pigeons than people, but you could just feel that something was going to happen."

The north wing of Union Station, leading to Beatrice Foods' Cold Storage center, which Dana renamed "The Ice House" and unsuccessfully attempted to turn into a design center. The building later was converted into residential lofts.

Meskis and Hickenlooper tried to buy Streetcar Stables but lost to Steve Owen. So they bought the Morey Mercantile building at 16th and Wynkoop streets. They also bought the building to the south, where they built 96 units of affordable housing, and a parking lot at 16th and Wazee streets. The book store conversion went relatively smoothly but building affordable housing was extremely difficult. Meskis called it "a major adrenaline headache." She said later that "historic redevelopment is hard to do without going high-end."

Despite the headaches, interest in the pigeon-filled warehouses was flourishing, and Mayor Peña, who supported the conversion of old buildings, became weary of DURA "demolishing into parking lots" what remained of LoDo. He and his staff developed a plan to save the rest of LoDo from the wrecking ball, but the seemingly innocent plan would grow into a highly controversial fight in City Hall.

Peña's planning director Bill Lamont, Historic Denver Inc. President Jennifer Moulton and others proposed to City Council the creation of a Lower Downtown Historic District covering 26 blocks below Larimer Street, with a primary purpose of prohibiting any further demolition of buildings without a compelling reason or purpose.

The fight over the proposal grew fierce. Dana Crawford, Bill Saslow and other developers who were already working in LoDo adamantly opposed it, even though Dana had founded Historic Denver Inc., and Saslow had served on its board. In essence, they felt they knew what worked best for individual situations, that they had already been doing a good job of preservation and didn't need a "one-size-fits-all" set of regulations.

"We all opposed an effort by the city to establish a historic district," Saslow said, "We were preservationists and very much in favor of saving the area. We opposed the specifics, like an edict that you can't tear anything down. It was overly restrictive. You couldn't even build a surface parking lot."

Others felt that LoDo should be cleared of old buildings and built anew. After months of fighting, city council was evenly split.

Early days in the revival of LoDo shows the original partners of the Wynkoop Brewing Co., standing in front of the building at 18th and Wynkoop streets in 1988. On the left is John Hickenlooper, who later would be elected to two terms as Mayor of Denver, then two terms as Governor of Colorado. To his left are Jerry Williams, Mark Schiffler, brewmaster Russ Scherer and brewery dog "Holiday."

Tom Gougeon, Peña's chief of staff, made a final appeal to council members, telling them the proposed new airport and proposed new convention center would be huge economic generators. But the vote on the historic district "would be the single most important vote they would cast on their time on Council," Gougeon said. "Half of LoDo had already been lost. Our belief was that downtown with a restored LoDo district would be an entirely different place than a downtown without the district.

"Much of the rest of downtown had evolved at that point to be mostly a 9 to 5 work environment. LoDo provided a character and fabric that downtown needed. LoDo had the potential to be a neighborhood and a destination. LoDo would also be the connection of downtown to the river through the redevelopment of the Central Platte Valley rail yards. It was a pivotal decision. We were either going to be more like Portland and Seattle, or more like Houston and Phoenix."

City council debated for five hours on March 1, 1988, then approved the new historic district by a margin of one vote.

"That was Tom Gougeon being a real visionary, way out ahead of most people," Hickenlooper said. "And he was right."

Hickenlooper gives Peña, Gougeon, Lamont and Jennifer Moulton credit for taking action, but he gives Dana credit for showing the city the value of LoDo's historic buildings, and the character, vitality and identity they would bring Denver once they were preserved and given a new economic life.

"We knew that without Dana Crawford, there would be no Wynkoop brewery. That building wouldn't be standing; someone would have torn it down," Hickenlooper said. "All those beautiful buildings would have been knocked over. Dana had the foresight and the appreciation of what those buildings had to offer that no one else at the time seemed to have."

·THE CENTRAL PLATTE RIVER VALLEY COMES ALIVE·

"This is completely non-salvageable. No one will live down here. I'll buy the dynamite and I'll push the plunger," *said friend and colleague, Jeff Shoemaker, upon learning Dana had purchased the concrete shell of a former flour mill to convert into luxury lofts.*

Dana did not start her real estate career as a preservationist. She was interested in the concept of "place-making," which, for her, happened to involve a group of historic buildings that needed preserving. She didn't restore anything; she renovated and repurposed a group of wobbly old buildings and turned them into a viable commercial enterprise. Before nearly anyone else in Colorado, she saw the potential of preserving older buildings—renovating them to modern standards then giving them new economic lives.

Following her success introducing Denver to "loft" living in empty warehouses in the early 1990s, Dana moved on to new projects. Her company, Urban Neighborhoods, purchased a string of five lovely Victorian-front buildings on Market Street between 16th and 17th streets, across from the transit district's underground bus station. Known as Market Center, the buildings housed primarily restaurants on the ground floor and offices on the 2nd and 3rd floors, which were finished with a décor of exposed red brick and wood beams. She moved Urban Neighborhoods into one of the 100-year-old buildings in the center for a number of years before she sold the complex in 1998.

In 1995, at age 64, Dana returned from a trip to Mexico and suffered a serious case of pneumonia, which caused some concern among her doctors whether she would survive. After many days in intensive care, and a long recovery at home, she regained her strength. (Dana would suffer one other serious medical setback, in 2008, when she received first an arterial stent, then a pacemaker in her chest. During the latter procedure, a surgeon accidentally sliced open her left lung. It took quite a while for her to recover from the setbacks.) The lengthy recu-

Original plaster castings inside Union Station.

peration from pneumonia served her well because, in 1997, she began a 10-year period of intense activity, completing some remarkable projects, as well as a few that were forgettable and one that never came out of the ground.

In October 1997, Dana announced her newest project, which many around her considered to be just shy of insane. She went north over 20th Street into a desolate, no-woman's frontier to purchase a graffiti-covered hulk of a gray, concrete former flour mill that had stood alone, abandoned and forgotten for 30 years. According to the National Register of Historic Places, it was built in 1906 by a cooperative of Longmont farmers, then purchased by J.K. Mullen's Hungarian Flour company After a series of fires, it was remodeled with designs from Frank Edbrooke, who had designed the Oxford Hotel and the Edbrooke loft building. The mill and its three attached silos had a thickness and strength that made the wood-framed Acme and Edbrooke buildings look puny in comparison. In the late 1960s, it was shut down, emptied of most of its heavy steel machinery and left to the pigeons, the homeless and graffiti artists. Architecturally and historically significant to the area, the concrete hulk was placed on the National Register, which some observers joked had been an unnecessary protection because it would be nearly impossible to demolish.

Dana's close friend and colleague, Jeff Shoemaker of the Greenway Foundation, attended the press conference announcing the project and fell into disbelief. "This is completely non-salvageable. No one will live down here. I'll buy the dynamite and I'll push the plunger," he told her. "It's right next to the main railroad line. I mean RIGHT next to it."

Shoemaker was right about the proximity of the rail line. The east edge of the mill's floor had a loading dock from which a forklift could reach into a parked boxcar for loading and unloading. Graffiti artists, who had covered every square inch of the concrete as high as they could reach, were able to stand on the loading dock and spray paint passing boxcars unnoticed. Dana just shrugged off the criticisms, until the building department refused to give her a building permit because the tracks were so close. That issue finally got resolved, quietly, and the $4.5 million renovation got underway. That figure was for construction only, not including the cost of the land, architects' fees, permits, financing, etc., according to Lisa Evans, the project manager who worked for Dana from 1997 to 2007.

The abandoned flour mill carcass north of 20th Street at Little Raven, which Dana renovated into 17 luxury lofts. Later she built a similar building in the rear, adding another 27 lofts, all of which sold quickly and continue to appreciate. It was one of Dana's most difficult renovation projects.

Photo: © Kim Allen, Denver Photo Archives

The mill was seven stories tall, with the attached silos each measuring 22 feet in diameter. Dana and architects Ann Cuthbertson and J.V. DeSousa began a clever, inventive and sophisticated conversion of an ugly concrete structure into elegant and tasteful residential lofts. Boldly, she left the concrete bare throughout the building, including massive posts holding 24-inch-thick beams 16 feet above the floors. Tin heating ducts and mechanical equipment were tucked high into the ceilings where possible but many of them remained in full view. She installed historically accurate windows, wood floors and elegant kitchens. Nearly every loft received a gas fireplace. The iron balconies were added years later.

Looking west out of the loft windows, the grassy City of Cuernavaca Park stretched from the Flour Mill 100 yards to the South Platte River. Dana saw it as an enormous front yard for the lofts. All seemed to be progressing nicely until the Denver Fire Department ordered a paved road be built around the circumference of the project in order for fire trucks to have access. Incensed by this intrusion, Dana called Mayor Webb.

"I remember this so clearly. Dana called me upset that the fire department was taking more of (Dana's land) to build a road. 'Mr. Mayor, this isn't right,' she said. 'The damn fire department wants this road around my building, taking away my property because of a damn fire truck. Why can't they just back the damn truck up?'"

Webb said he'd look into it, and asked the fire chief if they could back a fire truck up from the Little Raven Street entrance to the building. "I guess we could but it's not appropriate," Webb recalled him saying. "So we built it with a smaller circle in front so the fire truck could back up. It can't swing all the way around, but this made sense to me."

The 17 lofts sold quickly, averaging $150 per square foot in 1998. By 2015, most of the lofts had tripled in value, with a few increasing four times their original sales price. Dana chose for herself a 3,000 square foot, south-facing unit, with windows on three sides giving her an exceptional view of Coors Field, lower downtown and the orange "Travel by Train" sign atop Union Station. She moved in on Super Bowl Sunday, 1999.

"When I'm in there, I feel like I'm in an Edward Hopper painting," she told Westword.

The conversion was so successful that she built another building behind it, 10 stories tall and designed by architect Chris Shears to look like the original building. Construction costs were about $10 million, excluding land, architects' fees, financing etc., according to project manager Lisa Evans. Those 27 lofts, including a 5,400- square-foot penthouse, went on the market in 2001 averaging about $300 per square foot. They sold quickly and by 2015, were selling for an average of $450-$490 per square foot, roughly a 50% appreciation.

"She took a shell of vertical concrete, added an addition to the north and you can't tell the difference between the two," Shoemaker said.

Early construction of the newer building, with the original building on the left, facing east and looking out directly onto the railroad tracks and coal cars.

Southwest corner of the finished Flour Mill Lofts project.

Along the way to this success, Dana hit a snag with one of her closest friends, an event that gives some insight into how Dana has developed such a "tough" reputation.

Jill Crow moved to Denver in 1985 from Saratoga, Wyoming, where she had been raising her two sons on a ranch. She and Dana became close friends. They spent years together, laughing and drinking and riding around in the London taxicab. They traveled to Mexico, Italy and to Minnesota to visit Jill's family. The friendship became so strong that Crow was the first person to be called when Dana entered the hospital with a heart problem in 2008.

"We've had wonderful times together. I cherish her friendship," said Crow recently. "We've taken many trips together that were carefree and great fun. She's a great traveling companion, very curious and loves everything, even squid."

Crow loved the Flour Mill project, so much that she wanted to invest in it. "But we battled…it was my first encounter with the professional side of Dana. I brought in a lawyer, Gail Klapper, who determined that it wasn't a safe contract for me so I withdrew from the project."

But Crow loved the lofts so much that she bought a penthouse, not as an investment but as a place to live in. "She didn't deliver," Crow said. "I was promised two parking spaces in the front, without a column, which I never got, and a particularly large storage unit, which she gave away."

Crow never recovered from what she perceived as callousness on Dana's part.

"Dana is determined to have her way. She's unrelenting. Her friendships are swept to the side to achieve something. She tested my friendship. Today, I still feel that our friendship would lose over a business deal; she'd walk all over me."

Dana said she doesn't remember how the incident was resolved. But their friendship has survived, and remains on such good terms that the voice on Dana's cell phone message is Crow's.

In the midst of the Flour Mill project, Dana ventured east of downtown into the "Uptown" neighborhood, above Broadway between Colfax and 20th avenues, where she bought a red-brick apartment house, with lots of character and lots of pigeons inside. The Cooper Flats building on the northwest corner of East 18th Avenue and Logan Street had been empty for 22 years and had become an eyesore. Dana bought it in 1998, sensing that the neighborhood, within walking distance of the central business district, was about to take off. She converted the three-story building into 24 condos, meeting the city's requirement that 10 percent of the units would be priced as "affordable housing."

Once again, her vision of the untapped potential of a forgotten neighborhood was spot-on, and years ahead of the market. It took other developers another 8-10 years to understand Uptown's desirability. Today, the neighborhood is filled with boxy new apartment buildings, brick sidewalks, restaurants and coffee shops, primarily targeting trendy millennials who were born after 1980.

Bolstered with confidence from the success of the Flour Mill lofts, Dana stepped east over the railroad tracks into the area known as Prospect or the Bottoms, a rough industrial area and former home to many Italians, who worked in the flour mill, for the railroads and at the Denargo produce market. It sits west of Coors Field and north of 20th Street. For years, the notoriously flamboyant and uninhibited gay bar, Tracks, had flourished there, next to the railroad tracks, with an enormous outdoor dance floor and its thumping disco music out of earshot of the city. Much of the area had been torn down. Urban Neighborhoods Inc. bought 5.5 acres of barren land, without sewers, utilities or infrastructure of any kind. Dana envisioned rebuilding the area into an Italian-style village, with seven residential buildings encompassing a square or piazza with beautiful lights. This would be new development, without a hint of preservation.

Bill Mosher, who headed the Downtown Denver Partnership for almost 10 years, considered her move into Prospect as the "most inherently risky" and "most defiant of the marketplace" of any moves she had made before. Prospect was "nothing more than a hole in the ground," with no access, no drainage, no public improvements, Mosher said. "She's like a Whack-A-Mole, unpredictably she pops up somewhere else."

"She's like a Whack-A-Mole, unpredictably she pops up somewhere else."

She developed 49 units in the four-story Ajax building on Inca Street, the first of the seven buildings to be known as Prospect Place Village. Then she developed 60 units in the Jack Kerouac building at W. 31st Ave. and Huron Street, which was completed in 2006. But the Prospect Place project proved to be more difficult and expensive than anticipated. It also became enormously time-consuming, in part because of the lack of infrastructure and in part because of the city's new and untested requirement that a percentage of units be affordably priced. This drove the cost of the units higher than expected at the same time the market for new and relatively expensive condos was softening.

In 2007, Dana and her son, Jack, who handled the financing, decided to forego the remainder of their village and sold it to Trammell Crow Residential, which has since developed more than 400 units there.

Although the project ended flat for Dana and Jack, Mosher praised Dana's courage and vision. She couldn't finish what she had started, but better capitalized developers were able to follow her lead into the neglected area and they profited handsomely off of her vision.

"She jumped the tracks," said Mosher, who is managing director of Trammell Crow's operations in Colorado. "She straddled both sides of the tracks and developed them. I'll always look at Dana in terms of Prospect. A lot of other developers followed her there—the Garts, the Hirschfelds, Trammell Crow—she led the way and they followed her."

Part of Dana's genius was how quickly she grasped the value of preservation and how to make it work. Real estate development, from the ground up, would always interest Dana but preservation of the old would become her passion. From the moment she realized this in the 1960s in the middle of Larimer Square, Dana began seeing Denver with a different set of eyes. And that vision soon focused on Union Station, a gray, grimy eyesore that had lost its grandeur, its importance and its purpose in Denver's daily life.

Once the central hub for all rail transportation during Colorado's early years, with eight railroads bringing 80 trains a day into the terminal at one point, Union Station lost favor rapidly when airplanes began unseating trains as the main mode of travel. By 1980, only two scheduled passenger trains a day pulled into the forlorn station, not including the popular Ski Train that carried hundreds of skiers to Winter Park each Saturday and Sunday in the winters.

After Larimer Square's reinvention in 1965, there was little commercial activity of any significance below Larimer Street during the next 15 years. The Oxford Hotel came back to life in 1983, but staggered and stumbled through an awful economy for seven more years. Nothing else had much of a pulse.

> **"Everybody in the development business was going to the suburbs,"
> Dana said. "Infill wasn't even a word yet. Old Denver (families)
> didn't like preservation. But they liked it when it was done."**

Mayor Federico Peña was elected Denver's first Hispanic mayor in 1983, following his very successful campaign of "Imagine a Great City." Considered by many to be one of Denver's smartest mayors, Peña's administration quickly saw that the city needed more tax revenues; the city needed to be improved but there was no room to grow. The Poundstone Amendment had been voted into the state constitution in 1974 in order to stop Denver from annexing any more peripheral areas where white families were fleeing to in order to avoid forced busing of their school children. With no room to expand, Denver had to look inside its boundaries for taxable growth.

That's when Peña and his staff realized that the 4,600 acres of the Central Platte Valley contributed a measly $40,000 a year in property taxes to the city.

"I believed we needed to focus on developing large parcels of land to grow the tax base," Peña said. "In my first campaign speech, I told a group of business executives about redeveloping the Central Platte Valley, they looked at me (like I was fool). Half of them had never been down there."

Bill Lamont, Peña's planning director, developed a master plan for the river valley which included negotiating with eight railroads to remove more than 30 sets of tracks, leaving only two trunk lines. The plan called for removing the viaducts, or elevated roadways, stretching over the tracks and the river. They would be replaced by surface roads extending into the central valley in order to spur development. Peña got the central Platte valley cleaned out and ready for developers, but it took him until the end of his second term, when he left for Washington to become President Clinton's Secretary of Transportation and later Secretary of Energy.

Another goal of Peña's had been to move the convention center in the valley behind Union Station. But voters very fortuitously voted that plan down, so Peña tripled the size of the existing convention center from 100,000 to 300,000 square feet.

"Dana truly was a visionary. She set up historic preservation in Denver," Peña said. "There's no one else like her. She could be encouraging and extraordinarily supportive one day and challenge you the very next. She's one of the few who held on through the difficult times and she deserves credit for showing us the importance of historic preservation."

Peña's successor, Wellington Webb, who was elected Denver's first African-American mayor in 1991, liked Peña's plan, but made one significant and important change in the portion of the valley near Union Station.

"Trillium (corporation) owned the land from the river to about halfway in (behind Union Station), while the city owned the other half to the station," Webb said. "I flew with (state attorney general) Ken Salazar and (city finance director) Andrew Wallach to (Trillium's headquarters in) Seattle, and proposed a swap. I wanted the land from this (middle) point to the river and they could have the land from this (middle) point to Union Station. We agreed to the swap on a handshake that day."

"I'm a parks guy," said Webb. "I flipped the land to get the land next to the river in order to build a park...something special that would be remembered for generations. If you make the river your backyard, it becomes (a mess). But if you make it your front yard...for the apartments that were going to be built, they could walk outside to their park, sit on the river and enjoy it."

Webb and his planning director, the late Jennifer Moulton, planned out Confluence Park, at the confluence of Cherry Creek and the South Platte River; and the 20-acre Commons Park north of Cherry Creek, stretching along the east bank of the South Platte River to 19th Street. They also created the 35-acre City of Cuernavaca Park north of the 20th Street viaduct, from the Flour Mill lofts to the river. And they created these three parks without allowing a single housing unit to be built on such prime, waterfront land. In Webb's 12 years as mayor, he doubled the city's park acreage to 4,759 acres.

The Greenway Foundation, founded in 1974 by state Senator Joe Shoemaker and soon joined by son Jeff Shoemaker, began working with Webb and Moulton to clean up the South Platte waterway using public and private funds. The foundation also helped fund and build the extensive network of more than 100 miles of bike paths and walkways along the rivers. Dana was a founding board member of Greenway and served until the late 1990s. She has continued to work with Jeff Shoemaker, who took over the foundation after his father died in 2012.

Another thing that worried Webb was his fear that the major highways—I-25, I-70, I-225, I-270 and C-470—might be expanded to form a beltway around the city. Webb reasoned that a beltway would keep people from coming into the city. He wanted a transportation hub based in the center of Denver, with spikes extending out into the suburbs and beyond.

For that reason, he supported the FasTracks plan of building 122 miles of light-rail and commuter-rail lines from neighboring suburbs and towns into Denver. The Regional Transportation District, which operates mass transit in the metro area and had worked hard to conceptualize the FasTracks plan, liked the idea of making Union Station the transit hub for the area. At the same time, the private owners of Union Station, including railroad owners Philip Anschutz and Pat Broe, announced they were no longer considering redevelopment of the station, which had been deliberately excluded from the Lower Downtown Historic District, and offered to sell the station. In 2001, RTD bought

Union Station and nearly 30 acres of land surrounding it for $49.1 million. It later sold off portions of the land but kept sole ownership of the station and the 19 acres behind it.

Through an intergovernmental agreement, the City of Denver, the Colorado Department of Transportation and the Denver Regional Council of Governments bought into the master plan to redevelop the station and its surroundings. In 2004, voters in the eight metro-Denver counties approved a sales-tax increase to pay their share of FasTracks, one of the largest transportation improvement projects in the country, and the future was set. The FasTracks project ultimately is expected to carry a price tag of about $7 billion. The total remake of Union Station and the land directly behind it as the rail and bus hub for FasTracks is projected to cost $500 million in public funds.

Immediately, commercial developers sensed the changes that were coming and bought up nearly every square foot of the acreage available west of Union Station for commercial development. Total build-out of the area is projected to carry a value of more than $1 billion.

Plans for the renovation and reuse of Union Station itself remained separate from the transit improvements and commercial development surrounding the venerable structure. Once the passenger flow was designed for the station, a number of developers submitted proposals for redoing the station itself. With much difficulty and endless discussions, the list of contenders was whittled down to two finalists.

One was the partnership of Continuum and East West Partners, who were the major developers of the privately owned land west of the station. This group proposed a $25 million plan for converting Union Station into an office building, including a public market inside, similar to the Pike Place Market in Seattle.

The other finalist was the Union Station Alliance, a team of real estate people led by Dana and her partners. The alliance proposed a $38 million renovation which included a hotel, five restaurants, various shops, bars and "living room" furniture for the Great Hall. This plan would keep the station open 24/7 with much more access for the public.

The Alliance plan had many complex facets to it, so many that writing it strained the patience of almost everyone involved. Most of the details were hammered out in Dana's loft, where she had set up a bevy of workers to handle every detail. Dana ran the show, and stretched herself and her staff very thin.

Detail of the Lion's mouth on the front wall of Union Station, anchoring one of many support brackets holding up the massive metal and glass canopy over the building's entrance.

To draft a proposal for the project, the Union Station Alliance formed 7 teams. The architectural teams were Tryba Architects and JG Johnson Architects. The contractor was Milender White Construction Co., with general partner Ferdinand Belz III assigned to be the overall developer of the project. Larimer Associates would lay out all retail and restaurant spaces and Sage Hospitality was responsible for crafting the new hotel in the station. Dana, who was in charge of all interior design and decorations as well as the station's overall image, would be the project leader. A representative from each team met almost daily in Dana's office in her Flour Mill loft, where her staff spent an arduous month drafting the 100-page, highly detailed proposal.

The office frequently was chaotic because of the number of people working on such a large project, trying to bend so many conflicting opinions into a final plan. Dana, who was 80 at the time, had tremendous stamina, would work long hours and expected the same from her staff. Everyone acquiesced that she was the central figure and would have the final word on disputed details. All agreed that her clout would improve the team's odds for success in the competitive bidding.

But another cause of chaos was the fact that the office was in Dana's home, and sometimes she would have difficulty with boundaries, such as hosting dinner parties and asking her office staff to help with preparations, even the cooking. More than once, staffers would tend to the guests then be asked to clean up the kitchen. If Dana was too tired by the end of the party, she might send the staffers home but expect them to clean up the kitchen the next morning, causing resentment. Several of her close friends complained about the same lack of boundaries for them when invited as guests.

Being in control has always been important for Dana, going back to childhood. It's a common behavioral trait for a single child. But in the rough-and-tumble world of commercial real estate, the stakes are much higher; the foes much tougher, more sophisticated and certainly less forgiving of a competitor's mistakes. In her adult career, Dana learned to play hard ball as well as anyone; she learned how to defend herself, how to stand her ground with assertiveness and how to identify which battles to fight and which battles to avoid.

But as she matured in the war-like trenches of real estate development, a part of her remained vulnerable, unprotected and very sensitive to criticism, which is another, almost contradictory, trait of a single child. For instance, Dana has been in the local newspapers perhaps more than any other woman in Colorado. Early in her PR career, she sought out reporters and editors and learned about their craft, as well as their idiosyncrasies. She continued these relations throughout her career in real estate, and became close friends with several female reporters. Yet she never was able to grow a thick skin about criticisms of her in the newspapers, whether they were fair or unfair. Some stories felt like betrayals to her. Staffers said she would glean the papers for comments, letters to the editors and follow-up stories affecting her, wanting to know who was saying what about her. She shrugged off any talk about her thin skin, rationalizing that, "Newspapers can turn on you on a dime."

In certain areas, about certain subjects, she could become emotional, and vocal, either breaking down in sorrow or venting loudly in anger.

Throughout the interviews for this book, she teared up many times recalling difficult events of her past, and actually broke down crying on several occasions, such as when she was shown photos of her mother or lost friends. But her fiery temper came out as well. When this writer inadvertently learned of another book she was working on at the same time as this one and asked her about it, she responded in a fiery, volcanic outburst. Luckily, it died down almost as quickly as it erupted.

Young staffers, unaccustomed to such displays, would be terrified. "I had no idea what I was getting into when I started working there," said one 30-year-old woman who grew up rather privileged. "I was scared, intimidated. I really didn't want to disappoint Dana because of her reputation and all that she had accomplished. Every day, I would try to read her mind, try to stay ahead of her and anticipate her moods, which could change frequently. I knew if I showed any weakness, she would turn on me. The girl before me said she went home crying many times."

"Her strength? Her Type A personality."

"Her weakness? Her Type A personality."

One office manager, who worked eight years for Dana before retiring with her husband to Arizona in 2013, said she had had her differences with Dana but always admired her for her strength, her courage and her accomplishments in such a misogynistic industry. The manager's daughter has worked in Dana's office for a number of years, and her granddaughter continues to work there as a freelance graphics designer. Due to difficulties when the manager left, Dana requested that her name not be used.

"Her strength? Her Type A personality," said the manager. "She's a very strong woman, with great vision and a will to make things happen."

"Her weakness? Her Type A personality," she continued. "Right or wrong, you'll do it my way. She won't back down from a fight. And she's had many fights. For me, we would just agree to disagree, and that was fair for both of us."

———————————

Dana's team's proposal for Union Station included a 112-room hotel, five major restaurants, two eccentric bars, smaller food, ice cream and coffee shops, flower and book stores, and Dana's desire to turn the building's great hall into "Denver's living room," with couches, tables and WiFi hookups. In the center of the Great Hall, Walter Isenberg and Joe Vostrejs added two very long table shuffleboards, which have proven to be quite popular.

After a contentious fight that went on for months, RTD, on Dec. 20, 2011, awarded Union Station Alliance the rights to redevelop the station and gave it a 99-year lease, at a little less than $1 million a year based on gross revenues. Following news of Union Station's new planned hotel and restaurants, property values in LoDo jumped significantly, as much as 20-25% within a couple of months. Some property owners said buyers began walking the streets, knocking on doors with cash offers.

For the Alliance, complications soon popped up everywhere. For one, squeezing up into the attic of the old train station for the new hotel would require cutting dormers into the historic roof. That required approval of the National Park Service, the steward for registered historic buildings. The NPS also had to approve a $6 million historic tax credit, which was key to making the numbers work on the project. It took 12 months to work out the details, but it all came together: local architectural firms Tryba Architects and JG Johnson Architects delivered detailed plans for the renovation, permits were approved and the financing had been arranged with a local member of a nationally prominent investment family agreeing to loan the team roughly half of the project's construction costs. RTD separately was putting $16 million into the building for infrastructure and landlord/tenant finishes.

But even such well planned projects like this one are still subject to Murphy's Law, which says if something can go wrong, it will. With construction scheduled to begin in just three weeks, the financing fell apart, with the lender and the borrower blaming the other for the collapse.

Determined to keep the project alive, Walter Isenberg, Dana's partner in the Oxford Hotel and a general partner with the Union Station Alliance, called Chad McWhinney, a 40-year-old successful real estate developer with a growing reputation in Colorado. As a teenager, Chad and his younger brother, Troy, had started by selling strawberries from roadside stands in California. Their entrepreneurship expanded to real estate and then spread to Colorado, where they became master developers of Centerra, a $100 million mixed-use development covering 3,000 acres astride Interstate 25 on the east side of the City of Loveland.

McWhinney, who had known Isenberg and Dana for a number of years but had never worked with them, said he'd listen to a proposal about investing in Union Station. When did they want to meet? Isenberg, not wanting to sound panicked, suggested 7 a.m. the very next morning, Dec. 3, 2012, at the Delectable Egg in the 1600 block of Market Street. McWhinney said he already had a 7 a.m. meeting. Isenberg choked and suggested 6 a.m. McWhinney agreed, and showed up.

Over eggs, the partners asked McWhinney to put in roughly $19 million, or about half of the alliance's cost of $38 million to redevelop the station. McWhinney said he would run it by his younger brother and get back to them. How soon, they wanted to know? McWhinney said: "For the right opportunity, we can make a decision in five minutes." He called Isenberg that afternoon and said he was in, with certain conditions.

The next morning, McWhinney, his brother and their team met with all the Alliance members, and one lawyer, Bruce James. Dana and her partners listened to the group's conditions, then asked the McWhinney team to step outside of the room. The Alliance members talked among themselves for 30 minutes and accepted the McWhinneys' terms.

Top photo shows the myriad of documents needed to be signed to begin the renovation of Union Station. Believing that every document had been signed, the Union Station Alliance team members gathered inside the Oxford Hotel's Cruise Room bar to celebrate. In the lower photo, Attorney Elizabeth Paulsen, on the right, burst into the bar moments later to announce they had forgotten to sign the 99-year lease, perhaps the most important document of the entire project. Partners Chad McWhinney, left, and Walter Isenberg, center, sign the lease on the bar top next to an empty martini glass. (Photos courtesy of Chad McWhinney)

The final make-up of the Union Station Alliance LLC partnership included McWhinney, responsible for overall management of the Alliance, including finances and taxes; Isenberg's Sage Hospitality would manage the hotel; and Larimer Associates, in particular Jeff Hermanson and Joe Vostrejs, would manage the retail and food outlets including those in the Great Hall. Dana, with her vision and attention to detail, would oversee the interior designs, marketing and public relations.

Other members of the Alliance included contractor Milender White, the design teams Tryba Architects and JG Johnson Architects, and overall developer Ferd Belz, who had been involved in the development of Denver's Tabor Center.

"You forgot to sign the lease."

McWhinney said he had never seen such a large partnership use only one lawyer, Bruce James, of Brownstein Hyatt Farber Schreck. But he felt comfortable enough with James that he didn't bring in his own lawyers. On Dec. 21, 2012, everyone gathered in the Brownstein conference room and took two hours to sign "hundreds and hundreds" of documents. With the groundbreaking set for the next morning, everyone went to the Cruise Room bar in the Oxford Hotel to celebrate. With martinis sloshing over the rims at every toast, a young lawyer, Elizabeth Paulsen, ran into the bar waving a sheaf of papers. "You forgot to sign the lease," she yelled. Embarrassed but happy, the crowd bellied up to the Cruise Room bar and signed the single most important document of the entire project.

When the transcontinental railroads began to reach across the United States in the 1860s—Union Pacific to the north and the Atchison, Topeka and Santa Fe to the south—they avoided Denver because of the high mountains to the west. So Civil War Gen. William Palmer in 1870 built the Denver & Rio Grande Railway to run north-south along the Front Range between the two trunk lines, with stops in Denver, Colorado Springs and Pueblo. By 1881, Denver had eight railroads, each with its own tiny station. To consolidate them, the first Denver Union Station was built on land assembled by Walter Cheesman and partially financed by robber baron Jay Gould, owner of the Union Pacific Railroad. Fire destroyed the center structure in 1894 but it was quickly rebuilt. Rail traffic soon outgrew that station, so the much larger station we have today was built and opened in 1914. Designed by Aaron Gove and Thomas Walsh and made of concrete and Colorado granite, Denver Union Station is a prime example of the Beaux-Arts style of architecture, the same style (and age) as Grand Central Terminal in New York.

After the United States entered World War II, as many as 60 trains arrived in Denver each day, some of them commuter trains from suburbs like Littleton. One outgrowth of World War II was the development of air travel, which caught on rapidly. Stapleton Airfield east of Denver began luring away many train travelers. In 1954, the orange "Travel by Train" signs were added above the "Union Station" signs front and back, in an unsuccessful attempt to lure more railroad passengers. But passenger traffic steadily declined to only two trains a day by 1980.

Aerodynamic passenger trains of a bygone era line up next to the outdoor passenger platforms in the rear of Union Station.

*Early shot of Union Station looking southwest.
The elevated roadway is the 16th Street viaduct,
which was removed by former Mayor Federico
Peña. He also convinced the railroads to
consolidate more than 30 sets of tracks into two
trunk lines, freeing up some 4,000 acres stretching
down to the South Platte River. That set the
early stage for the redevelopment of the entire
Central Platte Valley.*

The original 65-foot-tall "Welcome" Arch in front of Union Station facing up 17th Street. The other side of the arch also had the word "Welcome", which confused departing passengers as they arrived at the station. Mayor Robert Speer changed it to "Mizpah", a Jewish biblical term asking the Lord to watch over travelers. The 70-ton iron arch, erected in 1906, became a traffic hazard as automobiles became more popular, and was removed in 1931.

A 65-foot-tall metal arch was built in front of Union Station in 1906. Weighing 70 tons, the arch had the word "WELCOME" imprinted across the top of both sides, illuminated by 2,194 lights. Almost immediately, the Chamber of Commerce questioned why the word "Welcome" faced up 17th Street, greeting passengers who were coming into the station to leave Denver.

So Mayor Robert Speer, who had had scrapes with Denver's Jewish community, changed the east side to read "MIZPAH", which the Book of Genesis defines as "May the Lord watch between me and thee, when we are absent one from another." Some local residents jokingly used to tell visitors that Mizpah was "an Indian word" for "Howdy, Partner."

Speer dedicated the arch "to stand here for ages, as an expression of love, good wishes and kind feelings…" But 25 years later, it was considered too expensive to light and a hazard to the growing number of automobiles. So it was torn down in 1931. Dana wanted to replace it after renovation of the station, but the estimated replacement cost of $2 million was too much. After some neighbors opposed the return of the arch, the plan was scuttled, including any talk of replacing it with a hologram. Instead, a sculpture with a brief history of the arch is being planned in its place.

A side view showing how the Mizpah Arch framed the entrance into Union Station. This photo, taken soon after the station was built in 1914, shows Union Station without it orange "Union Station" and "Travel by Train" signs up near the clock.

Interior view of Union Station before its renovation, looking west and north. The solid wall to the right of the benches is now the front desk of The Crawford Hotel.

Rows of wooden benches for waiting passengers. Aside from being very uncomfortable, the benches could not be saved during the renovation because they were lined underneath with asbestos to protect them from the heating grates in the floor.

During the renovation from December 2012 to July 2014, the exterior was washed, with all terra cotta repaired by hand. The large metal canopy in front was re-welded and re-glazed with wired safety glass, thanks in part to funding from Historic Denver Inc. The upper cornice of molded tin was restored and welded tight. All metal on the exterior, as well as light poles and bike racks, were painted "LoDo Green", a dark blackish-green found throughout the district.

Sadly, a 6,000 square-foot model train exhibit, which had been in operation in the basement since 1933, had to be dismantled and moved out to make room for mechanical equipment. The model railroaders have not found a new location, but the trains and villages are in safe storage.

In the Great Hall, the iconic wooden waiting benches had to be removed because they had been protected from the steam heating grates with a heavy lining of asbestos. Air conditioning was installed as were fire alarms and a sprinkler system. Six large, emergency smoke fans were installed in the ceiling, in case of a fire, to suck smoke out through perforations in the chandelier medallions and vents at each end of the ceiling. Fresh-air vents were added and four inches of acoustical plaster was added to the ceiling to improve the hall's acoustics.

The 65-foot-high ceiling is part of the city's ordinance requiring a line-of-sight view corridor down 17th Street from Broadway to the South Platte River. The large arched windows at each end of the great hall define the view corridor and nothing in that view can be taller than the window sills, at 5,209 feet above sea level. The view corridor west of the station is 160 feet wide, extending to the South Platte River. For that reason, the fabric tent over the rail lines was designed with a cutout to continue the view to the river.

The transportation portion of the project—the rail and bus lines, underground passenger walkways and the cut-out fabric roof—were designed by a team from Skidmore, Owings & Merrill, led by Derek Moore, a Denver native and East High graduate. Moore, the team's senior planner and one of the lead designers of the project, was a classmate with Jack Crawford at Dora Moore elementary and Byers middle schools.

"To come back to Denver and be part of this project, and to see what Denver has become, was fantastic," said Moore, on the telephone from his New York office. Now 58, Moore recalled when he was 10 or 11 years old working with Jack Crawford shoveling the squatters' rubble out of the Granite Building in Larimer Square shortly after Dana purchased it in the early 1960s. "It's amazing to think back when that area was Skid Row. Just look at it now."

Photo taken after the renovation, showing The Crawford Hotel sign.

Courtesy, © James O. Milmoe

Courtesy, © James O. Milmoe

Looking out of the central window on the east wall of Union Station, the view looks straight up 17th Street to Broadway. The window sill sits precisely at 5,209 feet above mean sea level.

Courtesy, © James O. Milmoe

Looking at the windows over the front entrance and the new Terminal Bar. Notice the elegant, post-Prohibition style Cooper Lounge on the mezzanine level above the clock. It's named after Colorado Gov. Job Adams Cooper, who served only one term, 1889-1891. A successful cattle rancher, lawyer and businessman, he built the architecturally significant Cooper Building at 17th and Curtis streets, which was the first building demolished by DURA in 1970. See page 158.

The plaster arches along both sides of the hall, which are outlined with 2,300 ornamental plaster columbine flowers—Colorado's state flower—were refurbished and painted. Original woodwork was stripped and refinished. Woodwork on the first floor is new.

Finally, the large, garish fluorescent chandeliers were removed and replaced with replicas of the original chandeliers. Using photographs from the Denver Public Library archives, designers from the AvroKO design firm, Tryba Architects and JG Johnson Architects designed replica chandeliers that are larger  than the originals and with some modern touches for better efficiency and brightness. Built by Project Light Inc., of Ohio, they were too large to fit through the doors and had to be assembled on-site.

The 112 hotel rooms fill the third floor and attic of the station. Off of the Great Hall are two wings, with 22-foot high ceilings on the main floor. Architect Jim Johnson squeezed a level of small sleeping rooms into the upper rear portions of the main floor of these wings. Dana designed them as Art Deco "Pullman" style sleeping rooms, each with a different railroad theme or motif. On the third floor, a new, structural floor had to be built to accommodate the mechanical systems. Much of the roof's structural timbers were exposed and 10 dormers were built to increase the natural light of the loft-style rooms in the attic.

The station opened unofficially on July 11, 2014, with a large, formal gala for hundreds of celebrants and well-wishers at $1,000 a head, all donated to area charities. Two weeks later, with the restaurants now operational, the station officially opened on July 26, 2014, exactly 100 years after the iconic structure had been built. The media swooned over the remake of Union Station. The hotel filled every room and the restaurants seated every table, and now have become so popular they are hard to get into. The Cooper Lounge on the mezzanine level is considered by many in Denver to be one of the ultimate spots for an after-work drink or a nightcap. In the Great Hall, Denver's "living room" has become a popular spot for the public to relax on comfortable couches and chairs; it's surprisingly civil, clean and well lighted.

A view of the original and refurbished wall sconces. Lining the interior of the building's arches are 2,300 plaster-cast images of a Columbine flower, Colorado's state flower.

The railroad clocks over the front and rear entrances are original, dating back to 1914.

Much of the station's woodwork was saved and refurbished, or reproduced to the original specifications of 100 years ago.

Dana accomplished her 50-year quest of "place-making" by creating Denver's finest public gathering space, something she first dreamed about while visiting New England town squares as a student at Radcliffe College. She also fulfilled a 50-year passion she had developed for preservation, by refurbishing the grande dame of Denver's historic lower downtown and revitalizing it by giving it a new economic life of its own. With her vision and tenacity, she had led the way. In gratitude and appreciation, her partners named The Crawford Hotel after her. During the frenzy to get the station open, her 83rd birthday had come and gone without much celebration. Now she was exhausted, so she took a long, pampered cruise in the Mediterranean with six friends.

Upon returning to Denver, she continued a hectic schedule of attending parties, receiving awards and accolades. Back at her desk, the pace continued. She began to spearhead a drive to improve conditions for the homeless. She lost out on a bid to redevelop the old Gates Rubber Co. complex on South Broadway. She and partners were purchasing and renovating single-family homes in the Villa Park neighborhood near West Colfax Avenue. She was buying and selling tracts of land in the River North district (RiNo) along Brighton Boulevard. In all, she had 11 projects on her desk. She wouldn't consider retirement, implausibly claiming with raised eyebrows, "I have to make a living."

She wouldn't consider retirement, implausibly claiming with raised eyebrows, "I have to make a living."

That comment might surprise many of her followers, who reasonably would expect her to have enough wealth to retire in luxury. Dana wouldn't discuss her financial worth. By all appearances, she's financially fit and comfortable but without the extensive holdings of the most successful real estate developers. In her lovely, expansive loft, she doesn't have the extraordinarily valuable art on her walls that some of her investors have hanging in their penthouses. She provides most generously for her extended family. She drives a reliable car. But there are no displays of great affluence or opulence around her.

In the capital-intensive business of real estate development, Dana hasn't accumulated the equity that would allow her to own a majority share, or even a large percentage, of her next project. Instead, she frequently relies on outside investors, some of whom have profited quite handsomely off of her vision and ideas.

"She's always been (annoyed) about not having enough money to invest in more projects," said Duke Crawford. "Especially for being such a visionary. If she had had more cash, LoDo would be even better than it is."

Part of the reason is that Dana's vision for new projects, like Larimer Square or loft living in abandoned warehouses, was so far ahead of the markets that she was unable to capitalize on the long-term appreciation of these successful projects. For instance, when she renovated the Edbrooke and the Acme lofts, she was forced by the lenders to pre-sell most of the units in order to get construction financing. Those same lofts 10-15 years later were selling for 300% to 400% more than she sold them.

Architect turned developer Bill Parkhill recently partnered with Dana on projects along Brighton Boulevard in the River North (RiNo) district. He considers her to be unique among developers in that she becomes very concerned with how a redeveloped building will fit into the city, even if means cutting some of the profits to do it correctly.

"Nobody's done more work than Dana Crawford. Nobody has the balls that Dana Crawford has," Parkhill said. "Her vision can be years ahead of the market." He pointed to her early ownership of the Oxford Hotel, which she bought into in 1980, then twice went into Chapter 11 bankruptcies (which she now refers to as 'Chapter 22') and only recently has started making a profit, a very healthy one at that.

"We have a saying that the pioneers get all the arrows and the settlers that follow get all the land," Parkhill said. "She's been so far out in front, taking all the arrows, while the people behind her came in and took the land. Almost everyone who has followed her has made a ton of money."

Walter Isenberg, owner of Sage Hospitality and a general partner with Dana in both the Oxford Hotel and Union Station, agreed with Parkhill: "If you want to make a lot of money, watch Dana. Buy as much of her projects as you can, then wait five years," he said.

Dana continues to work hard because of her passion for real estate and for preservation. She doesn't look back very often, and doesn't rest on her laurels. In fact, what legacy she will leave behind is the subject of many discussions. Many believe it will be Larimer Square, which started her march into preservation and honed her vision for saving the soul of Denver.

Her son Duke believes differently. "Union Station is the heart of her story. She's been on that project for 30 years. Her real strength came out in Larimer Square, but her legacy will be Union Station," he said.

Dana herself is conflicted, stating in an email that, "Loft living downtown was one of the most important milestones in the evolution of a great downtown."

But all of this comes up short. Limiting Dana's legacy to a collection of buildings, whether they are Larimer Square or LoDo warehouses or even Union Station, is too narrow. Dana's legacy will be her uncanny vision to see years into the future of a city's growth, her ability to identify new urban trends well before anyone else, and her unique talents to link the past with the future by preserving historic buildings while giving them new economic lives. That's exactly what she's done with Larimer Square, LoDo warehouses and Union Station.

Dana understood the concept of preservation as early as anyone in the nation. New Yorkers were forced to deal with the concept after their magnificent Penn Station was demolished in 1963. Mayor Robert Wagner, filled with regret, took only 18 months after that irreplaceable loss to sign the city's Landmarks Law in 1965, one of the nation's first measures aimed at historic preservation.

While that was going on in New York, Dana, in Denver, had already launched her plans to preserve the historic 1400 block of Larimer Street, in the heart of Skid Row. She had to push against the will of a majority of taxpayers who voted to raise their own taxes in order to pay to demolish much of downtown Denver. Dana's success in creating Larimer Square eventually gave Denverites a new sensitivity about preservation. With her influence, the Denver City Council passed its own landmark Preservation Ordinance, just two years after New York and years ahead of many major American cities.

Dana soon became a national leader in preservation. Eventually she was asked by 50 cities to help them sort out this mess of old vs. new and how to bring the historic sections of their communities back to life, such as Boston's Fanueil Hall, Underground Atlanta and the River Walk in San Antonio. Some of the most interesting cities in the country today are those that have made the link to their past, like New Orleans, Charleston, Savannah, Boston and San Francisco. Denver has been enriched beyond measure by the preservation of LoDo.

The National Trust for Historic Preservation acknowledged Dana's contributions in 1995 by bestowing on her its highest award, the Louise du Pont Crowninshield Award. In her acceptance speech, she told the distinguished crowd: "Denver has enjoyed a downtown revitalization that has reclaimed more than 40 individual buildings and an entire neighborhood of turn-of-the-century warehouses, now dubbed LoDo. Loft living in landmarks has become a solid part of Denver's residential real estate market in 10 short years. City leaders from all over the country have flocked to our historic doors to determine how we have accomplished so much in so little time."

Richard Moe, president of the National Trust for Historic Preservation, in his 1997 book, *Changing Places: Rebuilding Community in the Age of Sprawl*, praised Dana for the depth of her understanding of the complex nature of real estate: "She was more of a preservation-minded developer than a development-minded preservationist. She did not believe in preservation for preservation's sake, but as a means to other ends."

Colorado Gov. John Hickenlooper bought a warehouse in LoDo in 1988, then struggled to fill it.

"Dana had the foresight and the appreciation of what those buildings had to offer, that no one else at the time seemed to have," said Hickenlooper, who was an out-of-work geologist before starting the Wynkoop Brewery, then elected to two terms as mayor of Denver and two terms as governor of Colorado. "If she hadn't saved Larimer Square, urban (renewal) would have gone right down through Larimer Street and down into lower downtown. It would have knocked it all down. She single-handedly saved lower downtown Denver."

Bill Mosher spent about ten years as president of the Downtown Denver Partnership, one year as president of the International Downtown Association, then 15 years as a private developer and managing director of Trammell Crow's Denver office. He understands as well as anybody what makes a city an attractive place to move to.

"There are few cities in this world that have changed themselves the way Denver has. Denver is an urban story that is internationally important," he said. "Denver has no reason for all of this to have happened, except for leadership."

"Dana is a person who understands cities. I have no idea whether she's ever made money at anything," he said. "She likes historic preservation…in the midst of growth and change you preserve the past to tell a story. You're saving something but you're taking it in a whole new direction."

Denver has become a different city from what Dana Crawford found when she arrived 61 years ago. To a newcomer today, the city might seem attractive with all its new chrome and glass and construction cranes. But a deeper gaze into the city's soul shows an emotional connection with its past, with its foundation and its heritage. That emotional connection is what we value the most, because that's what gives great cities their character and strength and charm. Dana Crawford found that connection in Denver, gave the old a new life and in the process has given the city back its soul.

Dana Crawford waves her magical wand to unofficially open the renovated Union Station on July 11, 2014, to a crowd of friends, family and well-wishers who contributed nearly $1 million to attend the gala, all of which was donated to area charities. The station officially opened on July 26, 2014, exactly 100 years after the structure was built.

Education

Monticello College, Alton, Illinois
University of Kansas, Lawrence, Kansas
Harvard-Radcliffe, Cambridge, Massachusetts –
Business Administration Program

Development History—start dates

1965 Larimer Square
1980 Oxford Hotel
1990 Edbrooke Lofts
1991 Market Street Center
1992 Acme Lofts
1998 Cooper Flats Condominiums
1998 Flour Mill Lofts Phase I
1999 Flour Mill Lofts Phase II
1999 Prospect district
2000 Ajax Lofts
2003 Jack Kerouac Lofts
2012 Denver Union Station, opened July 2014

Businesses established

The Market
Antonio Tsai Chinese Restaurant
Victorian Jewelry Store
Crawford Department Store
The Cabaret
The Criterion
The Oxford Club Spa and Salon
Urban Neighborhoods, Inc.
Urban Neighborhoods Real Estate Co.

Civic Work

National

Board, National Trust for Historic Preservation,
1972-1981
Board, Project for Public Spaces, 1985-Present
Board, Preservation Action, President 1985-1987
Full Member, Urban Land Institute, 1981- Present
Honorary Member, American Institute of Architects

Colorado

Colorado Historical Society, 1983-2006,
Vice President Ten Years
Colorado Historic Preservation Fund Committee —
Ten Years
Colorado Preservation Inc., Founding Member
Historic Preservation Fund Committee,
1991-Present.

Denver

Downton Denver Partnership, Board and
lifetime member
Denver Art Museum, Board 1976-1982
Platte Valley Greenway Foundation, Founding
Member, Board 1974-1980
Denver Performing Arts Complex, Board 1994-1997
Historic Denver, Inc., Founding Member,
Board 1970-1980
Lower Downtown District, Inc., Founding Member,
Board 1984-1992
Downtown is the City Program, Chairwoman
1990-1991
Denver Center for the Performing Arts,
Advisory Board 1984-1990
Mayor's Housing Task Force, 1991
Friends of Union Station, Founding Member
Evil Companions Literary Award- Co-Founder
Union Station Advisory Committee (USAC)
Civic Center Conservancy

Awards

National Trust for Historic Preservation Louise du
Pont Crowninshield Award
AIA, Colorado Chapter, Honorary Member
University of Colorado, Honorary Doctorate
of Humanities
Colorado Business Hall of Fame
Bonfils-Stanton Foundation Award
Namesake, Colorado Preservation Inc.
Dana Crawford Award

Consulting

Albuquerque, New Mexico
Arvada, Colorado
Aurora, Colorado
Boise, Idaho
Brighton, Colorado
Broomfield, Colorado
Cedar Riverside, Minneapolis
Central City, Colorado
Commerce City, Colorado
Corning, New York: Main Street
Dallas, Texas
Detroit, Michigan
El Paso, Texas
Fort Collins, Colorado
Fort Worth, Texas
Greensboro, North Carolina
Hawaii, Statewide
Houston, Texas
Hutchinson, Kansas
Kansas City, Missouri
Mobile, Alabama
New Haven, Connecticut
Oklahoma City, Oklahoma
Omaha, Nebraska
Orange County, California: Laguna Niguel
Pittsburgh, Pennsylvania
Portland, Oregon
Providence, Rhode Island
Raleigh, North Carolina
Rochester, Minnesota
San Antonio, Texas
Savannah, Georgia: Broughton Street and City
Market
Seattle, Washington
Sheridan, Wyoming
St. Louis, Missouri: Laclede's Landing
St. Paul, Minnesota
Tacoma, Washington
Tampa, Florida
Tracy, California
Wichita, Kansas

BIBLIOGRAPHY

Buildings of Colorado, by Tom Noel. Oxford University Press, 1997.

Country Club Heritage: A History and Guide to a Denver Neighborhood, by Alice Millett Bakemeier. Country Club Historic Neighborhood Inc., 2000.

Dana Crawford: From Larimer Square to LoDo, Historic Preservation in Denver, by Dan Corson, Master's Thesis, University of Colorado at Denver, 1998.

The Death and Life of Great American Cities, by Jane Jacobs. Modern Library, 1993 edition.

The Denver Post, various.

Denver's Larimer Street, by Tom Noel. Historic Denver Inc., 1981.

Denver Renewed: A History of the Denver Urban Renewal Authority 1958-1986, by Donna McEncroe. The Denver Foundation, 1992.

Denver: The City Beautiful, by Thomas J. Noel and Barbara S. Norgren. Historic Denver Inc., 1987.

The Landlords, by Eugene Rachlis & John E. Marqusee, Random House, 1963.

Larimer Associates Collection, 1965-1985.

Molly Brown: Unraveling the Myth, by Kristen Iversen. Johnson Books 1999.

Murder at the Brown Palace, by Dick Kreck. Fulcrum Publishing, 2003.

The New York Times, various.

On the Road, Jack Kerouac. Penguin Books, 1976 edition.

Out Where the West Begins, by Philip F. Anschutz, with William J. Convery and Thomas J. Noel. Cloud Camp Press, 2015.

Rebirth of Union Station: A Vision for the Plaza, Project for Public Spaces Inc., 2005.

Rocky Mountain News, various.

Skyline, by Gene Fowler. The Viking Press, 1961.

Tastefully Yours: Savoring Denver's Restaurant Past, by Pierre Wolfe. 2002.

The Things That Last When Gold is Gone: Biography of Anne Evans, by Barbara Edwards Sternberg, with Jennifer Boone and Evelyn Waldron. Buffalo Park Press, 2011.

Timber Line, by Gene Fowler. A Comstock Edition, May 1977.

Women of Consequence: The Colorado Women's Hall of Fame, by Jeanne Varnell. Johnson Books, 1999.

"Zeckendorf" The Autobiography of William Zeckendorf, with Edward McCreary. Holt, Rinehart and Winston, June 1970.